The Totally Engaged Audience:

The Ultimate Guide for Fearless, Authentic & Engaging Presentations

By Marc W. Schwartz

Printed in the United States of America, Canada and the United
Kingdom

StarrComm Publishing – Ft. Worth, Texas

ISBN: 978-0-9981747-3-0

"Success is stumbling from failure to failure with no loss of enthusiasm."

Winston Churchill

TABLE OF CONTENTS

ACKNOWLEDGMENTS

Special thanks to my family, friends and business associates as well as my many teachers and mentors.

AUTHOR'S NOTE

For over 30 years, I have traveled the world presenting to, training and facilitating groups of all types. I've had the pleasure to present to groups large and small from Austin to Zurich. Over these many years, many places and many people, I've experienced a full spectrum of extraordinary outcomes and also embarrassing disappointments. In my youth, I was perplexed about life and its profound struggles. At age 26, I started a life-long strategy of interpersonal development. I wanted to understand why life seemed so difficult—why I constantly snatched failure from success especially in relationships, money and business. The lessons never seemed to sink in and the patterns repeated themselves in eerily similar fashions and in strangely predictable ways.

I listened to CDs, read books, attended seminars, studied successful leaders and even went so far as to "teach the concepts I learned." But little stuck and the struggles continued.

In my quest for personal development, I sat in many audiences and listened to many speakers, trainers and presenters. Some were effective and engaging. Most were not. The litmus test as to how engaged I was centered around how they made me feel in the moment and if they made me want to respond—with action. I became mesmerized by some people's ability to move and inspire me to positive action and tangible results, and I became equally fascinated by some people's inability (though intelligent, knowledgeable and maybe even well-spoken) to inspire me to do anything (other than wish I was somewhere else).

When I heard a good speaker, I listened, I learned and I acted. I watched many people present, speak, engage, rivet and captivate audiences. And it began to stick. I found my life's work. That's how I entered the presenting, facilitating and training world. I wanted to embed these lessons in my brain by repeating what I learned in order to save myself (and others) from wasted time, bad decisions and needless frustration.

Thus was born my passion, and from it came a mantra; the constant striving for the Faster, Better, Easier approach to speaking, engaging and moving audiences. Almost by accident, I began to do what I now urge, firmly believe in, and even sermonize about: Ask questions, good questions. They might seem like bad or good questions, right or wrong questions, easy or hard questions, but they must be asked. Ask many questions. Ask any questions. You won't learn much if you aren't curious and don't ask.

So I did. The first question: What knowledge, skills and abilities could I embrace to reduce my learning curve, conquer my fear and learn to engage an audience? Who does this well? Where are they? How do they do it? What lessons could I learn from the acknowledged masters (Zig Ziglar, Peter Drucker, Tony Robbins and Steven Covey)? What did they know that I needed to know to make my brain shift, my energy focus and my life work?

So I listened and learned and questioned everything. I was introduced to a world I was unfamiliar with but fascinated by.

Speaking publicly was nothing I ever envisioned for myself. Like a majority of the population, I had a debilitating fear of speaking in front of others. Yes, many studies have shown the average person fears public speaking more than death and roughly 25% of the population would rather die than speak in front of a crowd. Die? Wow!

I can't say I have ever felt that way about it, but I have had my moments. I remember speaking for the first time to a college political science class about a subject I had researched the previous night. I was woefully unprepared, the subject was difficult and my fear was crippling. If I'd been able to watch me the first time, I probably looked like a myotonic goat (when afraid, its body goes stiff and falls over, all while maintaining complete consciousness). As I walked to the lectern with embarrassing sweat stains clearly showing on my shirt, the best I could hope for that day was to be rendered rigid, fall face down and pray for unconsciousness. That didn't happen, but I was rendered rigid from the paralyzing fright. I made it through the speech and vowed never to speak in front of any group ever again. Ever!

At least that was my intention until my grandmother passed away six months later. I was assigned to give the eulogy my sister Jill had prepared. She, at the time, had an even greater fear of public speaking than I. My sister took great care in preparing the beautiful words and I loved my feisty little grandmother Maier, so much, I had to stand up, conquer my fear, and do the right thing: speak in public again.

But something happened.

3

On the day of the funeral, none of the typical fear, trepidation or nervousness engulfed me. I had a job to do and I was going to do it. I walked boldly to the front of the funeral parlor and spoke. What surprised me, and everyone listening, was my composure and presence. I felt calm. My sister had entrusted me with this task, I knew the subject well, and I realized I liked telling stories from my heart. And I was among family and friends of an adored woman.

It was a great joy to honor someone who meant so much to me in front of an audience. I felt an inner catharsis as I spoke and looked out at the warm but melancholy faces. I liked the look on the faces of the crowd who began to release the solemn, quiet sadness of the occasion as I spoke about my grandmother's beautiful life. It was an odd shift as I overcame that fear and dealt with the pain of the moment and engaged the audience.

I was hooked. Being authentic and speaking from the heart was exhilarating and a shift for me. But this acceptance, shift and process took time. I summoned the courage and found that moment to address an audience that wanted to hear my words. I didn't know why it worked so well back then, but I knew I took great joy in and from it.

After the eulogy and the funeral, I decided to pursue this as my life's work. I have given literally thousands of presentations over the last 30 years and have learned much. It has been a sometimes bumpy and difficult journey, but immensely gratifying and frankly, fun. So I decided to share what I have learned by capturing my journey in a book that would help others conquer fear and engage an audience. The old adage, "If I only knew then what I know now" applies.

It has not always been a linear process for me, meaning there has not always been a beginning, middle and end. Learning how to speak with confidence and engage an audience takes time, resilience, strength and yes, courage. So to make this process easier, this material is written in a linear fashion to help people new to this subject, as well as experienced presenters, to gain value. That is, when you must present to an audience, any audience, from two employees in a weekly meeting to 5,000 people at an international business conference, the process must be approached by first addressing the beginning (finding out you have to speak), then preparation, presenting, ending, aftermath and follow-up.

As such, *The Totally Engaged Audience* is written to easily accommodate you from the start...from knowing your engagement to speak, to the actual presentation, through the speech's ending, the afterwards and then the follow-up, all laid out on a linear continuum. It is designed so that the novice can glide briskly from chapter to chapter, and understand how to speak and communicate in an engaging manner. It is also designed for the public speaking veteran to drill down directly into challenging areas as a refreshing reminder. Written in a simple format to address each area, *The Totally Engaged Audience* moves in a time progressive manner, from beginning to end. It provides the simple but necessary steps to take to help your presentation shine and for you to achieve the true goal: An Engaged Audience.

There is a familiar old adage that applies to public speaking: (1) Tell 'em what you're going to tell 'em, (2) Tell 'em, and then (3) Tell 'em what you told 'em. I have expanded that adage to include a few more details in the process. The material will walk you through each step in the process of telling the audience like this:

1. *Preparing what you need to tell 'em*
2. *Tell 'em what you're gonna tell 'em*
3. *Tell 'em*
4. *Telling 'em through speech*
5. *Telling 'em via facilitation*
6. *Telling 'em by training 'em*
7. *Motivating them as you tell 'em*
8. *Problems and mistakes in telling 'em*
9. *Tell 'em what you told 'em*
10. *Telling 'em after it's over and remind 'em later what you told 'em*

As has been said by the greatest presenters of our time, "Often we learn more from failures than successes." This material will help you avoid some and hopefully most of the failures I have experienced, but not all of them. There is value in failing. Yes, failures are backhanded successes and some of the greatest successes were a result of real failures. These are harsh words to hear but necessary to understand.

This material will help you understand presentations via three types: Speech, Facilitation and Training. They all differ but are cumulatively presented because they are interwoven with each other. In order to "Totally Engage Your Audience", you must *educate* them, you must *train* them, and you must *entertain* them. Thus was born the concept I call, **"Edu-Train-Ment™."** Through the

"Edu-Train-Ment™" concept, you will begin to recognize the value of understanding these ideas, and their importance in conquering your fears, and being successful at any of these presentation types.

If you are like the average person who fears public speaking more than death, you can ease your fears by reading this book and following the processes described. I hope you enjoy the process as much as I do and the fearless victories you will have after reading this material, processing it, using it and achieving wild success.

Marc Schwartz

FOREWORD

I have known Marc Schwartz for more than fifteen years now and have worked with him in several areas including training and presenting. Not only is Marc an excellent and knowledgeable teacher, he is a dynamic speaker. I am always amazed by how effectively and effortlessly he engages audiences and connects with them.

Marc is a "get it done faster, better and easier" kind of guy. He doesn't waste time on trivia or more details than his audience needs to get a powerful result. I found that same approach in reading this book. It is full of really useful information that is sure to propel you to new levels of effectiveness and proficiency as a public speaker without all the boring minutia so many other how-to guides contain.

The Totally Engaged Audience is comprehensive and impactful enough to encompass virtually every essential facet of speaking—gaining confidence, developing poise, getting and holding the attention of an audience, and inspiring them to action. Yet it is also brief and precise enough to use as a quick reference guide as you develop your own unique style.

If your work requires that you speak in public or your heart is tugging you in that direction, you are going to love this book.

Enjoy!

Dr. Sherry Buffington
Presenter, Trainer, Consultant and Author of:
Who's Got the Compass? I Think I'm Lost!
The Law of Abundance
Exiting OZ,
and *Power Shift: The New Rules of Engagement*
(Co-authored with Marc Schwartz)

SECTION I:
When You Have To Speak

Chapter 1:
Preparation

Before you tell 'em

So, you have to speak in front of people. You've been in-formed you have to present something in front of an audience of people staring at you, waiting, wondering and hoping to hear something interesting.

Oh my! Panic and fear grips you by the throat. What do you do? What do you say? What do you wear? What do you talk about? How do you do this? Holy cow!

These are all valid questions. But questions steeped in fear; the primordial DNA strand that keeps us from being eaten by ani-mals. Before you tell your audience anything, let's start at the beginning and calm the situation. These are not wild animals; just ordinary people like you who want to hear what you have to say. Yes, they want to hear what YOU have to say, and believe it or not, they are probably a little afraid as well.

"THE ONLY THING WE HAVE TO FEAR..."

So first, address your fear. This is the most important thing you can do to engage any audience. Relax.

Fear is a human emotion that is intrinsic in our DNA. It is a natural reaction to anything that might harm us. Fear can be a great motivator, a powerful ally and a horrible enemy. So first, acknowledge the fear and realize that it is the emotion that will help you get through this new task. Not only that, it will be the emotion that helps you succeed.

According to Dr. Sherry Buffington, there are three obvious types of fears we all experience:

1. Ridicule
2. Rejection
3. Embarrassment

Each of these fears has specific triggers, but they can all be overcome by understanding their root cause, present importance and future solution.

There are several things you can try yourself to minimize fear and I present my preferred methods here. The first one is a do-it-yourself method called Emotional Freedom Technique (EFT) for which I provide detailed instructions on how to use it. You might want to try this first; and, if it doesn't do the trick for you relatively quickly (in a few minutes), I suggest you invest in something more powerful.

Below the EFT method, I have provided information on two very powerful methods that get right to the core of whatever holds you back and eliminates the issues almost immediately. These two methods are facilitated, but they need to be. It's like the difference between applying a bandage to a minor wound (which we can all do for ourselves) versus having heart or brain surgery. For the deeper more complex issues, it's wise to put yourself in the hands of a trained expert. In my opinion, the two facilitated methods presented here, CORE MAP and RAMP (Rapid Accelerated Mind Patterning), are the holy grail of personal improvement. They get amazing results and produce rather miraculous transformations even where other methods have failed.

EMOTIONAL FREEDOM TECHNIQUE

EFT is based on the discovery that imbalances in the body's energy system have profound effects on one's personal psychology. Correcting these imbalances, which is done by tapping on certain body locations, often leads to rapid reduction in stress. By rapid, that means **stress can vanish in minutes!!!** EFT focuses on the body's subtle energy meridians. Simply stated, it is an emotional version of acupuncture, except needles aren't necessary. Instead, you stimulate well-established energy meridian points on your body by tapping on them with your fingertips.

Use EFT prior to any program, especially if you're stressed or out of flow. It's a simple and fast way to let go of stress and be present and focused on the audience.

> *"THE CAUSE OF NEGATIVE EMOTIONS IS A DISRUPTION IN THE BODY'S ENERGY SYSTEM."*
>
> **GARY CRAIG, EFT CREATOR**

Tapping on designated points on the face and body is combined with verbalizing the identified problem followed by a general affirmation phrase. Combining these ingredients of the EFT technique balances the energy system and appears to relieve psychological stress and psychological pain.

Each EFT tapping exercise consists of a **SETUP** Statement, followed by two rounds of tapping the sequence of **8 EFT** body points. **ROUND 1** focuses on the problem by repeating the *negative reminder phrase* while **ROUND 2** focuses on the solution by verbalizing preferences, choices and possible alternate outcomes.

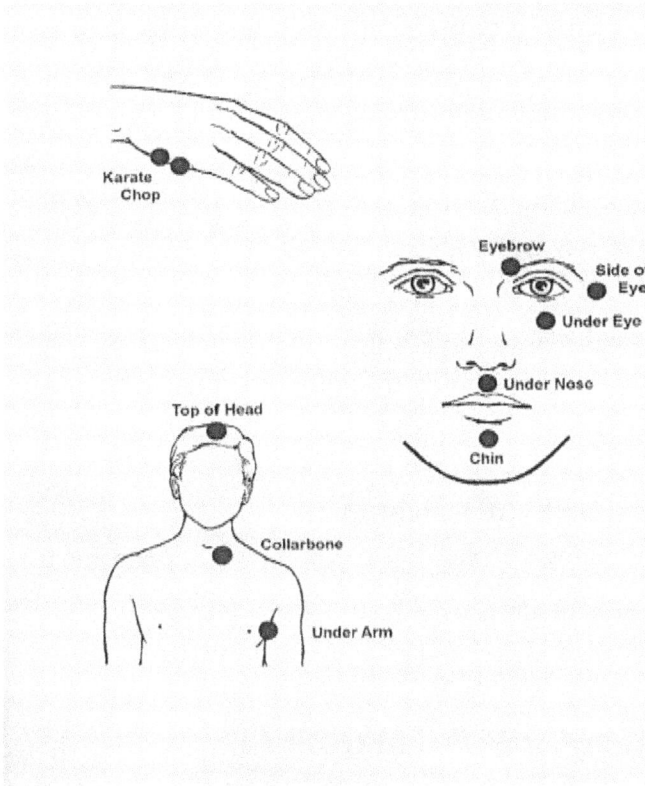

SEQUENCE OF TAPPING POINTS

1. Eyebrow
2. Side of Eye
3. Under Eye
4. Under Nose
5. Chin
6. Collarbone
7. Under Arm
8. Top of Head

SETUP STATEMENT

- Rate the intensity of the issue being addressed on a scale of 0-10

  - 10 = strong discomfort
  - 0 = no discomfort

- **Tap the karate chop point** on either side of your hand continuously while repeating the entire set-up statement 3 times for that issue.

Example of a SETUP Statement:

"Even though I have this fear people will reject me if I present in front of a group, I'm learning to deeply and completely accept myself."

NEGATIVE TAPPING SEQUENCE

- Starting at the eyebrow point, begin tapping each point in the sequence of points approximately 7-10 times while repeating the negative reminder phrase.

Example of a Negative Reminder Phrase:

"I am afraid people will reject me if I present in front of them."

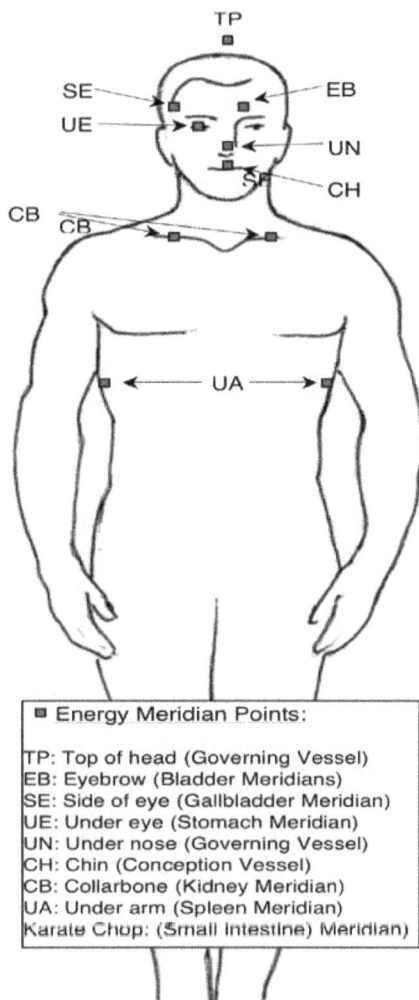

TP

SE   EB
UE   UN
          CH
SE
CB
CB

UA

■ Energy Meridian Points:

TP: Top of head (Governing Vessel)
EB: Eyebrow (Bladder Meridians)
SE: Side of eye (Gallbladder Meridian)
UE: Under eye (Stomach Meridian)
UN: Under nose (Governing Vessel)
CH: Chin (Conception Vessel)
CB: Collarbone (Kidney Meridian)
UA: Under arm (Spleen Meridian)
Karate Chop: (Small Intestine) Meridian)

POSITIVE TAPPING SEQUENCE

• **Starting at the eyebrow point again,** tap each point 7-10 times while repeating the sequence of **8 positive phrases**.

• This allows you to install what you would prefer to experience emotionally in your thought patterns and in your life.

Example of 8 Positive Phrases:
- Eyebrow – to feel acceptable now
- Side of Eye – accepting success
- Under Eye – release the need for other people's approval
- Under Nose – appreciate who you are
- Chin – to feel acceptable inside
- Collarbone – accepting success no matter what others think
- Under Arm – opening all channels for success
- Top of Head – appreciate how worthy you are

DEEP BREATH

• Slow deep breath to move the energy through your body and further anchor your preferred thought patterns

Fear is a necessary, unavoidable and natural biological response to a new situation. Fear helps us survive difficult situations. Fear is an early warning system that protects, but it also says something to you that might surprise you: "Hey, opportunity is knocking. Answer the door." Banish your fright and embrace your courage.

> *"MOST PEOPLE WOULD PREFER TO BE LYING IN THE CASKET RATHER THAN GIVING THE EULOGY."*
>
> **JERRY SEINFELD**

TWO ADVANCED SOLUTIONS FOR DEALING WITH THE FEAR AND BLOCKS THAT HOLD YOU BACK

CORE MAP (CORE Multidimensional Awareness Profile)

This is an advanced assessment to help you discover how all the years of conditioning have altered the true self you came into the world to be and quickly move you past any negative conditioning so you can step out and shine authentically. Some of the conditioning we receive as children is beneficial. It enhances our natural abilities. Some of it, in fact most of it for the majority of people, suppresses our natural abilities and unless we can see what has been suppressed and what has not, we don't know what to work on. Many people spend an entire lifetime searching for their truth and die without ever knowing the joy of living their life authentically. CORE MAP gets beneath the mask we don as children and gets to the core truth. When you know what your core truth is, you can step onto any stage or enter any arena stronger and more confident. What you will learn about yourself and other people through CORE MAP can help you connect to and better understand any audience; and more than that, it can connect you to the fullness of life. You can learn more about CORE MAP at www.energyofsuccess.net.

RAMP (Rapidly Accelerated Mind Patterning)

If fear or anxiety is what prevents you from stepping out there and doing what you want to do, nothing will eliminate either or both of them faster or more completely than RAMP. This is a method that is almost 100% effective at removing limitations and knocking out mental or emotional blocks that keep you stuck. RAMP can accomplish more in a single hour than other methods accomplish in months and even years. RAMP works even where "tried and true" methods, such as traditional therapy, have failed. The transformation is immediate and once a desired change is made through the RAMP method, it occurs effortlessly and remains permanently. After RAMP, people regularly report that where their automatic responses used to frustrate them, they now delight in them. That's the power of this amazing method. To learn more about RAMP, go to www.energyofsuccess.net.

YOU TALKING TO ME?

Now about those audiences we fear. Who are they and what do they really want? This sounds obvious, but knowing the audience is one of your best strategies to make the job easier. Here are some questions to ask:

- How many?
- What age?
- Gender mix?
- Demographics?
- Education?
- Experience level?

Understand why your subject is important to them. What do they expect from the presentation? The audience is probably nothing like you thus asking questions and learning about them can help you connect. There are few things more embarrassing than providing simple information to a knowledgeable audience, or speaking over the head of an audience that is new to a subject.

Having done a great deal of speaking in foreign countries myself, I have found it vital to understand, for instance, the cultural differences of the audience. What do they wear? Do they appreciate humor? What gestures are appropriate?

Before the speech begins, research your audience. Ask the organizer or sponsor of the meeting and find out the experience level and the audience expectations. And know the potential types of audience.

There are four types of audiences based on their desire to be there:

1. **Captive Involuntary** – They are there because they have to be, likely don't want to be.
2. **Practical Pragmatists** – They are there because they need to be, and know they might benefit.
3. **Committed Serious** – They are there because they want to be, and will benefit.
4. **Socially/Financially Motivated** – They are there because they really want to be there, and are aware that it might even change their lives.

Which audience are you speaking to, and how motivated are they?

The Captive audience will need some humor, movement and plenty of interaction.

The Pragmatists will likely be slightly bored and maybe jaded, but are aware of the importance of the presentation.

The Committed audience will know the importance and will be eager to learn. They will need more hard information and less gimmickry.

The Socially/Financially Motivated audience will be eager to hear the presentation and will be ready to act. This audience often needs to be tamed to temper the overzealous, for fear that the real message of the presentation gets lost in the raw enthusiasm.

When you understand and study your intended audience and their expectations, you can structure your presentation through the lens of Edu-Train-Ment™ to make it more appealing, effective and engaging. Your audience will be more gratified and you can enjoy the appreciation, applause and adulation afterwards.

GREETING

Often reliable information is not available on your audience, so an effective way to understand a smaller audience is to greet them at the door. As they walk in and you introduce yourself, ask brief questions about their background, experience, education, location, etc. This also serves to assess the age and gender mix of the audience. In addition, people like to be greeted and welcomed. It can be a positive warm-up to the event and you might even make a friend.

LOOKING GOOD, BABY

Know this: You will be judged by how you look. So, this is the easiest thing to control and almost impossible to overcome if it's not handled appropriately. First impressions will decide how well you will be received and sadly, often the only thing that will be remembered. Any audience forms an impression before a word is uttered. Here are a few tips on what will be noticed:

- Clothing should reflect the formality of the event. Business casual is acceptable in most speaking engagements.
- Clean shaved faces are always acceptable for men. Facial hair should be groomed.
- Nails are clean and manicured.
- Hairstyle is pleasant and appropriate to the audience.
- Makeup is used in a proportional and appropriate way.
- Jewelry is distracting and judgments are often made based on quality and brand. Use sparingly.
- Polished shoes – nothing worse than great clothes and bad shoes.
- GUM – get rid of it. I've actually witnessed presenters chewing gum during a presentation.

Personal appearance is frequently an overlooked part of presentation skills and audience engagement. It is *you* in the spotlight. It is *you* that they are looking at and before you open your mouth, judgments good and bad, are being formed.

Visual impressions are as important as verbal impact, and much easier to control. Pay close attention to appearance.

ROOM TO ROAM

Be familiar with the speaking venue layout. Visit the location prior to the meeting to see how the room will be laid out. Get comfortable with the surroundings, size, setup, lighting and acoustics. Stand at the podium, move around on the stage, speak, yell and listen, and seat yourself in some of the chairs to gauge the view of the audience.

This will help to calm your nerves and remove any unwanted venue surprises. It will also give you information to plan the next step: the Entrance.

Chapter 2:
Entrance

Preparing what you need to tell 'em

So now you've been informed you will be speaking. You have dutifully arranged your thoughts. You have carefully researched your audience. You have visited the space where you will speak. So you're all ready to go, right? No, not yet.

Part of preparation for engaging an audience is to make sure you are mentally prepared for what is about to take place. And just as important is the actual entrance and introduction to the engagement.

To ensure that the beginning goes smoothly, it is vital to have already warmed up the body and brain, established credibility with the audience, walked through a pre-speech ritual, prepared a proper introduction, used an artful opening and drawn the audience in with a hook.

WARMING UP THE BRAIN

Pre-speech rituals are essential to successfully engaging an audience. Just like any athlete does stretching and warming up for optimal performance, the speaker must engage the same

pre-speech routines. Since ultimately it is the mind that is the tool for the speech, it must be ready.

Clean the room first. Mentally and emotionally "clean the room." Since everything in public speaking is about energy, stack the deck in your favor to cover everything that could affect an audience.

Visualize a whirlwind of white light in the room sweeping through and picking up all distractions, bad situations or negative energy. Picture a waterfall flowing into the room with its fresh clean, crisp waters washing away all the negative energy and leaving a fresh, clean and open space.

This is a commonly used technique, but perhaps it is not your style. If not, think of your own way to prepare the energy you'll need to engage the audience. How you choose to warm up your mind and make it ready for the task is up to you. But liberate yourself from fear by making your brain visualize energy, success and a positive outcome. It works.

WARMING UP THE BODY

Motivational speaker, Tony Robbins, has enough energy to keep 4,000 people engaged for 50 hours over four days (and probably a small city's electricity grid if he chose to). His pre-speaking ritual involves incantations, affirmations and movement—lots and lots of movement. This makes sense since one of Robbins' core teachings is that energized movement can change your state of mind. Robbins gets himself in the zone for about ten minutes prior to taking the stage. He jumps up and down, spins around, fist pumps, stands with his arms outstretched and even bounces on a trampoline.

As a presenter, physical preparation will boost your energy significantly and make a huge impact on the way your audience perceives you. It's important to adopt some sort of physical pre-presentation ritual since movement and energy are intimately connected.

Carmine Gallo, a Speech Coach and Author of *The Presentation Secrets of Steven Jobs,* explains a technique used with executive speakers over the years and it works. Right before the presentation, ask the speaker, "On a scale of one to ten—one being asleep and ten being Tony Robbins who is yelling, fist-pumping and smacking his hands against his chest—where are you right this second on the energy scale?" The typical response is somewhere between four and six. I then suggest the speaker clap his or her hands together three or four times, shake out their arms, and put a big smile on their face. "Now where you are?" Ask them. "About seven or eight," the speaker normally responds. "Good enough to engage. Now rock it!"

This simple exercise results in dramatic changes. In fact, the typical speaker stumbles a few times as soon as they begin presenting. Why? Because they have been forced out of their comfort zone on the energy scale. But as they practice at their new energy level, everything changes—their body language, eye contact and delivery.

ENERGY TRUMPS TECHNIQUE

Come from a place of authenticity, care about and focus on the audience and bring a high level of passion and energy for the material. The audience will be much more forgiving and open, even if you're not technically perfect. Preparation and practice are necessary. Know that technical imperfections will be overlooked if the message and value has been delivered with good intention and authentic passion.

Energy improves technique and more importantly, it overcomes mistakes—and mistakes will happen. As a speaker, you are being judged on the quality of your story, your body language, and your delivery. Raising your energy level to a "7 or 8" will help to improve two of three qualities—body language and delivery. Practice the ritual before you try it in front of an audience. It will take you out of your comfort zone until you get used to your new energy level. The right energy level is critical and will overcome mistakes.

THE CREDIBILITY FACTOR

The audience will want and need to know something about you to help achieve authenticity. They have chosen, for whatever reason, to attend this event and to hear you speak. And they have a powerful reason for doing so—your credibility.

In advance of the presentation, the audience should be informed about you, why you are the speaker, and what you have to offer them, teach them or give them. Ensure that somehow they will know what you bring to the table. It will make the job much easier and the message more effective.

THE INTRODUCTION
Grab control immediately and don't let go because you only have a few seconds to make a good first impression.

Take the approach that this audience is in your house. When people come to your house, there is a certain experience and sense of respect you want them to feel. It is up to you to make that happen by keeping a healthy balance of control without stifling the environment. Introductions are etiquette—making people feel welcome, respected and comfortable all the while keeping interest and curiosity engaged.

SET THE CONTEXT EARLY
Engage the audience first, and then tell them your name and why you're here.

Engage early and often! Within the first 30 seconds, ask a question or get the audience to interact with one another in some way. "How many of you would like to learn something new about _____. If you could have fun while learning, would you be open to that?"

Energy, presence and focus—if you're boring or unsure within the first minute, it will take time to earn the audience's attention again, if it can ever be earned. Audiences read energy and make judgments about the speaker quickly. The sooner the logical left-brain questions are addressed, (as in "What's in this for me?"), the sooner the audience can become present and engaged.

UNPLUG

The sooner we answer the audience's logical left-brain questions about why they should listen to this or "What's in it for me", the sooner we help the audience unplug from their mental mind talk and emotional barriers about why they should be somewhere else.

Unplug them. Ask, "How many of you are here against your will or how many would rather be somewhere else right now?" The sooner you bring attention to the mental 800 lb. gorilla, the sooner they can let it go and go about the businesses of engaging and learning.

Help them answer the question foremost in their minds about what will be the specific benefits they will gain in return for their time and presence here today.

Audiences judge us within 30 to 60 seconds! That's it. The greeting is valuable time that we cannot retrieve. So, grab it and make it matter.

Chapter 3:
Hook

Tell 'em what you're gonna tell 'em

The hook is the launching point for your presentation. It is the statement that summarizes the importance of the speech and the creative grabber that draws the audience in and allows you to engage them.

> "If you want to speak and be heard, it is essential to place your message in an emotional narrative that will be easily stored in someone's mind and easily recalled later."
>
> **GREG POWER**
> **– PRESIDENT,**
> **WEBER SHANDWICK**

But first, what exactly is a hook and how is it done? Simple. It is that flash point utterance that seizes the mind of the listener. It is that one bold statement that brings the eyes and ears in the room to you. It is not the introduction. It is the answer to the audience-wide query: "Why am I here?"

How is it done? There are actually many ways to do this so here are a few suggestions that can be used to hook the audience:

THE STORY

"Have you heard the tale of the _____?"

The resonating power of stories cannot be understated. People love stories, especially those tales centered around personal experience. Stories can be a powerful teaching tool and spark the imagination, stir the emotions and leave lasting impressions. They inspire, teach, and even heal. It doesn't matter if the stories are old favorites or ones about you. Stories provide a powerful trigger to create a new perspective or forge a metaphor for deeper insight.

Stories teach lessons and provide a bridge between key concepts and implementation. Here are a few quick points to remember:

- Make sure stories support and apply to key presentation points.
- Better too short than too long.
- Personal stories are better than telling other people's stories.
- Body language can make the story fun and compelling.

THE JOKE

"The Past, the Present, and the Future walk into a bar...it was tense."

Use humor if you want people to listen. Humor is one of the most powerful tools in your arsenal when it comes to engaging an audience. Use jokes, cartoons, videos and light-hearted, self-effacing statements about yourself. The best source of humor is the audience. Get one or several people up to engage in an exercise. Do a demonstration on strength and muscle testing and it's almost guaranteed to get a laugh, especially when you ask for the biggest, baddest and meanest person in the room. It's a great oppor-opportunity to do improvisation.

TIP: One of my favorite general humor openings is the robber story: *Man walks into a convenience store and pulls a $20 bill out of his pocket and asks the attendant for change. The attendant opens the cash drawer and the customer pulls out a gun and says, "Give me all the money!" The store attendant gave him all the money. The robber runs five blocks away and starts to count his money and realizes he left his original $20 bill on the counter. He counts his money and realizes all he got was $15 (a net loss of five dollars and a net gain of years in prison.) "How many of you think the robber is in the wrong business?" Or, "Do you think he needs some coaching around his chosen line of work?"* It gets a laugh, lightens the mood and provides an opening to tie in to any number of points.

CAVEAT: When in doubt, leave it out. Let's face it some people are really funny and some people are just, NOT. If you're not comfortable using humor, then don't. Use funny videos or car toons to do the work for you. The best humor that gets the best response is humor about yourself (something embarrassing always works). Always test to make sure it is a simple and a relevant humor pertaining to the point of the speech. Unless you're doing a late night standup comedy routine at a local comedy venue, leave the questionable and dirty stuff out. There is always risk in using humor. You might think it is cute or funny, but some may not. The upside is minimal and the downside is huge.

THE PICTURE

Fun, interesting and humorous graphics can get people's attention and help to set the tone of the presentation.

THE BOLD STATEMENT

The statement of fact is always a grabber.

The entire current population of Earth could fit inside Texas, and it would still be less crowded than New York City.

THE QUESTION

"Are you sick and tired of being sick and tired?"

The audience will always answer it inside their heads.

THE QUOTE

"When you're going through hell...keep going." Winston Churchill

Everyone likes to relate to someone they've heard of. They will picture the person and respond.

THE SOUND

The sound of music, children and explosions will always grab attention and set the mood.

THE STATISTIC

"25% of people surveyed would choose death over speaking in public."

Be sure to back up the statistic with a source for reliability and accuracy.

THE EXPERIENCE

"I never knew how good I could be until I was really bad."

Like stories, sharing experiences draw in the audience and provide a personal connection to the subject matter.

THE MAGIC

Go to local magic store and get several beginner-level tricks to learn and use with groups. Hokey tricks can work against you, but fun and imaginative magic tricks are always attention grabbers.

THE SKIT

A good short skit can often be a great way to make a point or use humor. Challenge groups to create skits around key points, if they are a crowd that would respond well.

THE VIDEO

YouTube is a treasure trove of visual anchors and entertainment for reinforcing key points, but keep it brief.

THE CHARACTER

Create fun characters to give a different perspective.

Willie B. Lively
Elder
Entrepreneur

Marco The
Mediocre Magician

The Great
Swami Bubba

The hook is the rocket launcher for the presentation. Each one of these mechanisms can be used to lure in the listeners, affirm the message and hook the audience in order to confirm that what is about to be delivered will be worthy of their time and valuable to their lives.

A great hook can launch you on your way to the three basic kinds of presentations: The Speech, the Facilitation and the Training.

SECTION II:
The Show

Chapter 4:
Speech

Tell 'em

So now it's time for "the show." That is, you are now expected to deliver information in the form of a presentation. In order to properly prepare for your presentation, it is absolutely critical that you know what type of presentation you will need to deliver (they are not all the same). Though there are variations, the three main types of presentations are:

1. **SPEECH** – This is the most straightforward of presentations. It is typically one person speaking with little or no interaction between the audience and the speaker. It is also commonly referred to as a lecture, a keynote, an address, a performance, or just a talk, and rarely lasts more than 1-2 hours.

2. **FACILITATION** – The facilitation encompasses all things that are in a speech but differs from the speech primarily in that it is a dialogue. That is, there is generally regular interaction between the audience members and the speaker in the form of comments, questions or even speaker-to-participant interviews. Facilitations tend to be lengthy, and may exceed one day, but there is no rule of thumb for length.

3. **TRAINING** – Training encompasses all of the above. It will almost always include a monologue or lecture, address, or speech; it is going to include plenty of audience interaction; and it is going to teach a great deal of information to an audience that will require every faculty of engagement you possess. Like a Facilitation, Training will be lengthier and can easily exceed one day, depending the subject matter.

SPEECH

A "Speech" is typically a one-way street. You are passing on, in verbal form, a slice of your genius to an audience who will watch and listen, but probably not interact. It is at its core a one person, singular speech: A monologue. And yes, it can be lonely and scary up there.

In light of that, the Speech is not unlike an actor's audition, or even a live performance on stage. There are listeners who are waiting for you to present words and impart knowledge to them that will somehow sway their opinions, make them learn something new, or just process information that will affect their lives.

As such, the Speech will need to be handled in much the same way as a stage rehearsal, audition or an actor's performance.

Every actor dislikes auditions. It's awkward, intimidating and nerve-racking standing in front of one or several strangers and pouring out your soul for a role. A Speech is not unlike an audition, but it is live, and there are no "do-overs." You get one chance and the audience will judge you based on that one take. So it is essential to practice, and even test it on a friend or family member(s).

But it is also a great opportunity to shine and prove your mettle. You can be unique. That time is when you're allowed to do a Speech. This is a rare opportunity to actually make the choice yourself on exactly what you'll be saying and what message you want to be delivered.

Here are some ways to handle your Speech. These tips will help you engage your audience when it is just you alone, standing up there on stage under the bright lights, getting to say whatever you want:

1. Choice

Choose the material for your Speech carefully. If you have the time for research and practice, take it. It will make you a better presenter. A good Speech will allow you to impart a wide variety of information: stories, statistics, trends, events, etc. Choose one that complements you and your unique knowledge and abilities, and allows you to shine.

2. Act As If

Even if this is your first time speaking to an audience, act like you know how to do this and that you know the rules. It might sound obvious, but sometimes pretending you know what you're doing becomes a self-fulfilling prophecy. Yes, you can become good at this monologue thing, even if you have to fake it a little bit.

Standing straight, looking people in the eyes and smiling always adds to professionalism. But most importantly, pretend you are comfortable, even if you're not. People will notice your outward signs of confidence, even if the inside is a raging tidal wave of fear. You can "fake it till you make it." It is just a matter of time until you will exude on the outside the inner calm inside.

3. Energy and Movement

Give off energy in the Speech. Given that there is little or no direct dialogue with the audience, this makes for easy boredom and droopy eyes. Counteract the solo nature of the act by giving the eyes of the audience something to follow: Your energy and your movement.

Too much energy can be distracting, but you won't find any audience who thinks that not enough energy is better. Having to slow down is better than having to step it up. Keep the energy up, but the volume appropriate. Changing the pitch and volume of your voice can add to the energy.

Whether you're on a stage or in a smaller office, move around. When you're passionate about something, you move, and that needs to be reflected in your monologue. If there's a section of the Speech that is serious and requires reflection, then use sincere eye contact to convey the mood. It will add to the meaning and punctuate a point. Be mobile.

4. Face Everyone
Face forward unless you are moving to the sidewall. Give them your profile if needed, but be brief. If you follow the previous tip, you'll obviously be walking around, but keep your focus forward most of the time, toward those you're speaking to.

Even if the Speech is intended for one person, which some are, don't ignore anyone. It's all too common for a presenter during a Speech to focus on one person in the audience who seems intently interested in the subject. It will make others in the room feel ignored and the one focused on person will feel uncomfortable.

Give the Speech as if you're talking to a group of family, neighbors or friends sitting in your living room. Make eye contact with each of them, if possible. Look closely without staring. You're talking with them and to them, not necessarily at them.

5. The Sound of Silence

Oh, by the way, SHSHSHshshshsh! Sometimes silence is golden. And silence is powerful. Allow learning to occur through the power of silence. Don't be afraid of silence. No need to feel compelled to fill all the auditory white space with words or noise. Something happens when the surroundings are quiet. The mind slows down.

There is space available to organize thoughts and for new ideas to surface and become permanent. The subtext of silence can be powerful.

6. On Messing Up

If you screw up, just press forward. Remember what Winston Churchill said? "When you're going through hell...keep going."

They probably won't know you messed up. People in real life mess up when they're talking, so if you keep going, they'll think you're a great speaker and that was part of the Speech. Act as if everything went as scripted and don't be overly apologetic, as it will draw attention to a mistake they may not even know you made. They probably won't know the difference and they probably don't want to either. Forge ahead after flubs.

THERE IS ONLY ONE YOU –
HONOR THE AUTHENTICITY.

"We have to dare to be ourselves, however frightening or strange that self may prove to be."

MAY SARTON

There are as many types of presentations and presenters as there are people in the world, so the key to standing out and making an impact is being you. Being authentic is the key to tap into the rich human reservoir of natural talent and energy each person has available to them, so the audience is more likely to remember you and your message.

TIP: Be the "guide on the side" vs. "sage on stage." Even if I'm doing a keynote address, I like to keep this axiom in mind. It pays to be humble. Remember, we are there for the audience. We are there to give them value, knowledge and benefit. If the audience gets what they want and need, the meeting planner/coordinator will get what they want and we all win. We, as presenters, are not always the most important person in the room. The audience ALWAYS is.

TALE: I remember a keynote I did many years ago for a group of association executives. My plan was to come out in costume, say a pithy line while taking off the costume in front of the group thus driving home my point about change in their industry. I was a little nervous about how this was going to go down given it was my first time to do a live costume change. All was good until I was introduced and walked out on stage and FROZE. I mean stone cold forgot my lines and stared at the audience for what seemed like an eternity (3-5 seconds).

In those 3-5 seconds, I actually considered running off the stage and going home so as not to suffer the further humiliation of blowing a high visibility opportunity with this client. Instead it came to me to ask a question of the audience which pertained to a common pain their industry was suffering through. The question seemed to hit home as their body language indicated contemplation. Whew! This gave me time to think! I asked another question which seemed to tap into real energy as I heard a large percentage of the group verbally agree. These questions did three things: Got the group engaged, gave me some credibility for knowing their industry pain points AND gave me time to settle down and re-connect to my planned opening lines which eventually went very well.

Chapter 5:
Facilitation

Telling 'em through facilitation

The Facilitation is a dialogue. The Speech is a monologue. Though these basic differences seem simple, they are not. *Facilitate is* defined basically as "to make easy." This is a simple definition but not an "easy" achievement. Facilitation mastery takes practice, a lot of practice.

BASICS

Just as a traffic cop controls the flow of moving vehicles for safety of travel, a good facilitator controls the flow of moving information to the audience for safety and understanding. The facilitator's tool kit is a set of techniques, knowledge and experiences, which they apply to protect the process the group is working through. The process is how the group goes about accomplishing their task. The facilitator helps to create the process, adjust it, keep it heading in the right direction, and most importantly, keep the audience attached and engaged.

RESPONSIBILITIES

1. Intervene if and when discussion veers off course.
2. Identify and control dysfunctional discussion.
3. Inclusion of everyone.
4. Summarize goals and outcomes.
5. Close the meeting with actionable results.

CHALLENGES

1. Managing conflict.
2. Maintaining focus.
3. Simplifying information dump.
4. Handling misperceptions and emotion.
5. Develop the audience so they can work without a facilitator.

BEGINNING

Most people are nervous about speaking to groups as well as being in new groups. Begin the Facilitation by walking around and meeting and greeting as many as possible and briefly visit with them in a light-hearted way. This simple act immediately begins to relieve any fears, both yours and theirs. It allows you to establish getting connected and creates an initial level of trust.

INTRODUCTION

All presentations need an introductory segment. The form this takes will depend on the facilitation design and your facilitation style. The introductory segment can include:

- Introductory remarks.
- Hook (State clearly what's in it for the audience. Ask questions.).
- Acknowledge group for their participation.
- Explain role as facilitator.
- State the purpose.
- If an agenda is used, explain it.
- State desired outcome for the facilitation.

THE ABSOLUTE POWER OF QUESTIONS

Dr. Sherry Buffington recently said that if a person really hears a question, then "the subconscious wants completion on the question and does not like open loops." When a question is posed, engagement increases based on the desire for completion.

He, who asks great questions, wins. The human brain pays attention to questions. Questions are a built-in audience engagement tool. The subconscious is unable to <u>NOT</u> pay attention to a question. It will always seek closure. So, make questions the foundation on which you build your Facilitation.

Begin the discussion with a summation of the topic and a starter question or statement. Examples:

- *"What is the difference between ..."*
- *"Who can tell us about ..."*
- *"What would you do if ..."*
- *"There are over 300 million people in the U.S. Why do we always ..."*

Your role during a group discussion is to facilitate the flow of comments from participants. Although it is not necessary to inter-ject your comments after each participant speaks, periodically as-assisting the group with their contributions can be helpful. Here are tips to help you facilitate group discussions:

Move the discussion forward by using more starter questions or by asking follow-up questions. Some examples of follow-up ques-tions are:

- *"What else can we add to that?"*
- *"Does anyone disagree? Why?"*
- *"Who can give us an example of that?"*

Avoid closed-ended questions that can be answered with a "yes" or "no." They discourage rather than encourage further discus-sion. You can do this by summarizing the main points and then asking, "Can anyone add anything to that?" or "Are there any other ideas or thoughts?" or "What are we missing here?"

Tony Robbins discussed the value of questions. He said, "The qual-ity of your life is in direct proportion to the power of the questions you ask. Learning to ask empowering questions, especially in mo-ments of crisis, is a critical skill that will ultimately shape the meaning you create and therefore the quality of your life."

SAFE

The audience wants to feel emotionally safe in the environment you are facilitating. It is up to the facilitator to set up the envi-ronment, which we call the "Container." "A 'Container' is a vessel, a setting in which the intensities of human activity can safely emerge. The active experience of people listening, respecting one another, suspending their judgments, and speaking their own voice are four key aspects of creating the Container for dialogue." (*Dialogue: The Art of Thinking Together* by William Isaacs)

The Container provides an energetic and safe setting in which honest speech and creative transformation can take place. The Container provides people with a measure of psychological safety. It is always my goal to create the Container early and often until I can sense some level of trust within the group. In small groups, I contribute to this by asking for interaction and affirming the participants. In large groups, this may be less likely so I rely on visualizing and energetically "cleaning" the room before I start.

Set the container and create safety for shifts, transformations and learning to take place.

I truly apologize for not creating a container of safety in my opening remarks
and I'd like to note your continuous improvement as a team

ENGAGEMENT

Achieving a "Totally Engaged Audience" means it must be done frequently. Engage participants often. Keep people guessing when they will be called on to speak or act. Keep the audience present to keep them engaged by these tasks:

- Read something short and interesting.
- Ask a follow-up question, such as, *"What do you think is the most important part of this list?"*
- Elaborate on a thought.
- Use a flip chart.
- Let an audience member lead an exercise.
- Put audience into separate groups and give each group a task to perform.
- Role-play in front of the room.

NAMES

Use participant names often.

- People love to hear their names. This is an incredible rapport builder.

  "To build on what Stacy said…"
  "Jack, what do you think about…?"

- Even in a large group, asking people their names then using it with earnestness, sends a message of connection.

OBJECTIVITY

Be an advocate for furthering the dialogue by being objective. Try to keep your opinions to yourself. If participants feel you have the answer up your sleeve, they'll be thinking about what you want to hear, not about what they think. Your role during group discussion should be more as an "advocate for further thoughts" than a teacher of information (Speech).

WRITE

Write down key points or new ideas as the dialogue progresses. This will help you keep the discussion on track and remind you later of points that bear inclusion in the discussion.

SUMMARIZE

Summarize the main points of the discussion. This will reinforce learning and ensure understanding. You may want to have a member of the group do the summary if you feel it will encourage a quiet individual to join in more. Summarize (and record, if desired) the major views of the group.

Example: "I have noted four major reasons coming from our discussion as to why managers do not delegate: (1) lack of confidence, (2) fear of failure, (3) comfort in doing the task themselves, and (4) fear of being replaced."

Pull together ideas, showing their relationship to each other.

Example: "As you can see from Dan's and Jean's comments, personal goal setting is very much a part of time management. You need to be able to establish goals for yourself on a daily basis to more effectively manage your time."

BALANCE

In Presenting It's All About Balance		
PACE	*Too slow*	*Too fast*
INTERACTION	*Too cooperative*	*Too competitive*
TONE	*Too serious*	*Too playful*
IMPLEMENTATION	*Too rigid*	*Too loose*
SHARING	*Too intrusive into personal feelings*	*Too protective of personal feelings*
FOCUS	*Too much focus on results*	*Too much focus on the process*
CONCERN	*Too much concern for individual*	*Too much concern for the group*

REINFORCEMENT

Relevant tie-ins or references should be reinforced. Years ago, I took groups through outdoor challenges. I learned about the power of tying in the physical experience to relevant life or business issues. Helping people create mental bridges between the experiences and the practical application can be a real challenge if not planned for and reinforced periodically. Open discussions either in a full group or small groups is helpful and forges the point to be discussed.

Stumping the audience is a fun reinforcement technique. Break the group into teams of 4-6 people. Have them elect a spokesperson and select a team name. Ask 5-7 questions from the previously covered material and indicate that only the team spokesman can raise their hand and answer for the team. Each correctly answered question is a reward to the winning team after each round. This is an excellent way to review information by tapping into the naturally competitive nature of the group.

CHECK-IN

Check in periodically with the audience and see where they are and what things are/are not sticking. Typically I'll ask the group to take a deep breath, hold/release and then do a quick review. Ask the audience to review what was covered:

"Where are you with this information?"

"In what ways can this information help you do your job better?"

"What does / does not make sense?"

"What confuses you?"

"What part(s) of this information could you start using immediately?"

"Based on this information, what will you start, stop or continue doing?"

Most people will agree "they got it" and will "start using it immediately." People don't like to appear slow. This is why I start early, in any session, building the container of trust and reinforcing it throughout so people will (hopefully) feel safe to tell the truth if something is holding them back.

EXCITE

Show excitement. Body language and vocal tone make up the heart of speech. If you lack passion and commitment to your material, the audience will mirror that. Even if you are a highly visible expert with huge successes but come across with an air of egotism and indifference, this will kill your ultimate message. "People don't care how much you know, until they know how much you care." Get real clarity around your personal intention and "why" you are doing this.

Energize a discussion by quickening the pace, using humor, or, if necessary, prodding the group for more contributions. *Example: "Here's a challenge for you. For the next two minutes, let's see how many ways you can think of to use two of the concepts we've covered so far."*

PARAPHRASE

Paraphrase what a participant has said so that he or she feels understood and so the other participants can hear a concise summary of what has been said.

Example: "So, what you're saying is you have to be careful when conducting a counseling session to avoid using inflammatory phrases like 'you always' or 'you never.'"

CLARIFY

Check your understanding of a participant's statement or ask the participant to clarify what he or she is saying.

Example: "Are you saying this approach is not realistic? I'm not sure I understand exactly what you meant. Could you please share it with us again?"

COMPLIMENT

Compliment an interesting or insightful comment.

Example: "What a good point. I'm glad you brought that to our attention."

AFFIRM

People seek affirmation and do not want to be wrong. An audience member will go to great lengths to be right, especially in front of others. So, find something good in every response by affirming the answer.

"Thanks for sharing that."
"Good insight."

Even if you get a totally wrong answer, you can always find something good.

"OK, good thought…and how about_____?"

Nothing about this makes the person wrong. It provides a quick transition to the best answer.

ENCOURAGE

Keep 'em talking. Opposite of the Pattern Interrupt (covered on page 44), how can you encourage others to talk more, especially when you know or think you know they have something valuable to say. Some of my favorite encouragement phrases are:

"Tell me more."

"Can you elaborate?"

"Go a little deeper if you will."

"Share a little bit more about that."

ELABORATE

Elaborate on a participant's contribution to the discussion with examples or suggest a new way to view the problem.

Example: "Your comments provide an interesting point from the manager's perspective. It could also be useful to consider how a sales rep would view the same situation."

DISAGREE

Disagree (gently) with a participant's comments to stimulate further discussion.

Example: "I can see where you are coming from and I'm not sure what you are describing is always the case. Has anyone else had an experience that is different from Jim's?"

MEDIATE

There are frequently strong opinions expressed in any facilitation that require mitigation. To keep any negative energy level in check, mediation is often necessary. It can be a delicate balance. Mediate differences of opinion between participants and relieve growing tensions.

Example: "I think Susan and Molly are not really disagreeing with each other but are bringing out two different sides of this issue."

TIP: I tell everyone before every session to please turn off phones, put them away and get rid of computers unless we are using them for an exercise. Inevitably someone will pick up their phone and check messages or texts during the program. When I see them doing this, I go stand right next to them and ask a question about the material we just covered. Doesn't take too long before the unspoken message to the group is, "If you don't want to get chosen at an unprepared moment, then leave your cell phone off."

ONE FINAL NOTE:

THE POWER OF QUESTIONS

The raw power of questions cannot be overstated. They are the driver of all successful facilitations. My father had a huge influence on me when it came to my speech style. He often said, "*A man will be infinitely more successful by learning to ask good questions and sincerely listening to what people say.*" He contended you should listen as much, if not more than you speak and those who learn how to ask questions are in control of the conversation.

From the book, *Power Questions: Build Relationships, Win New Business, and Influence Others*, Andrew Sobel and Jerold Panasv contend, "Good questions are often far more powerful than answers. Good questions challenge your thinking. They reframe and redefine the problem. They throw cold water on our most dearly held assumptions, and force us out of our traditional thinking. They motivate us to learn and discover more. They remind us of what is most important in our lives."

In my experience, the ability to ask great, high value questions is a key foundational skill for both Facilitation and Training. I regularly hear from participants after they go through one of our coaching training programs, about the fabulous conversations they are also having with their teenagers. I ask them how the 4S Conversation and Coaching model we teach made a difference and it seems to come down to sincerely asking questions and really listening. This is a wonderful by-product of corporate training that has helped thousands of managers create more effective conversations with their team.

THE TWO MOST POWERFUL AND EFFECTIVE SKILLS YOU HAVE AS A FACILITATOR ARE YOUR ABILITY TO: ASK QUESTIONS AND LISTEN CAREFULLY!

Facilitations are not easily mastered, but if many of these methods are employed, Facilitations can be one of the most gratifying presentation types you will undertake.

Chapter 6:
Training

Telling 'em by training 'em

Training sounds easy, right? Training just sounds simpler and less involved than it really is. Training (teaching) involves all of the previous skills required in Facilitations and Speeches and a few more. Training is a monologue, a dialogue and a great deal of balancing and juggling the two simultaneously, and then making them work effectively to teach a skill or impart important information.

So, the previous items mentioned in Speech all apply: Choice, professional acting, energy, movement, facing the audience, staying fresh, getting close, the importance of silence and finishing strong.

The rules of Facilitation also apply: The importance of questioning, making the audience feel safe, engagement, saying names, objectivity, balance, summarizing, checking in, showing excitement, clarification, complementing and mediating disputes.

Training is the combination of the two presentations and deftly handling them to achieve "competence." But before Training can be assimilated and effectively employed, we must first back up a little and understand the concept of "competence."

Initially described as "Four Stages for Learning Any New Skill," the theory was developed at Gordon Training International by an employee, Noel Burch, in the 1970s. (It has also been attributed to Abraham Maslow, although it does not appear in his major works.)

THE FOUR STAGES OF COMPETENCE

1. **Unconscious incompetence**
    A person does not understand a subject and does not recognize their lack of competence. They may even deny the importance of the subject. <u>You don't know what you don't know.</u>

2. **Conscious incompetence**
    A person does not understand something, but recognizes the deficit, as well as the importance. <u>You now know what you don't know.</u>

3. **Conscious competence**
    A person understands or knows how to do something. Demonstrating mastery of the skill or knowledge requires intense focus and involvement. <u>You know what you know, but still have to think it through.</u>

4. **Unconscious competence**
    A person has so much practice with a skill that it is now

ingrained enough to be performed with ease, without careful concentration or deep thought. In fact, it can now be performed while executing another task. It can now be taught to others. <u>You know what you know and don't have to think about it. It is second nature.</u>

The mastery of Training is achieved in the 4th stage. This does not mean Training can't be conducted in the 3rd stage, it is just much more effective when "unconscious competence" is attained.

By combining the skill sets necessary in a Speech and a Facilitation, the presenter will have the basics required for conducting a Training. But there are nuances that will need to be mastered in order to achieve the "unconscious competence" we desire to be able to perform a Training.

TRAINING AND LEARNING

True learning is a five-phase process. You can't apply all five in a short presentation; but if you also train, you will need to find ways to incorporate all five to be effective. There are five phases to integrated learning: (1) Impact, (2) Repetition, (3) Utilization, (4) Internalization, and (5) Reinforcement. All five are essential for real learning to occur. When you incorporate all five effectively, your audience will be able to put what you deliver to use immediately and they will retain and utilize it over the long term. The following illustration presents the learning phase of a five-point model used by the corporate training company, Star Performance Systems. It shows the five aspects and the effect of each on learning.

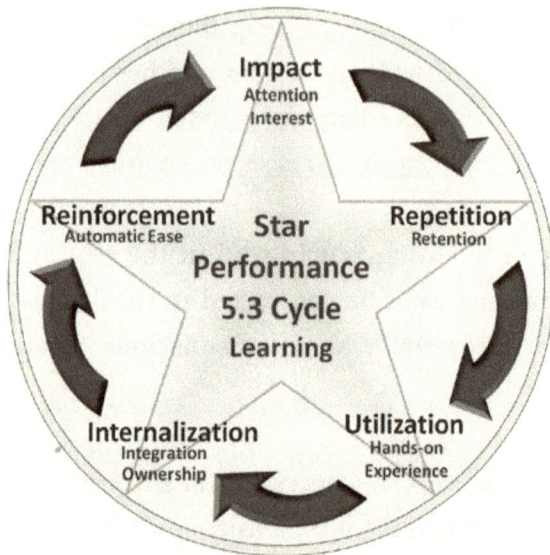

Star Performance Systems, Dr. Sherry Buffington (2013)

Ester Buchholz writes in (1998) *Psychology Today,* "Solitude is required for the unconscious to process and unravel problems. Others inspire us, information feeds us, practice improves our performance, but we need quiet time to figure things out, to emerge with new discoveries, to unearth original answers."

TALE: I've been part of a strong international men's group for many years; and several times a year, we convene to do a three-day weekend training to teach other men how to be in service to self, family and community. In the process, we do a number of targeted exercises and subsequent debriefs. One of the most powerful aspects of the debrief section is called the "burn-in." In essence, after an exercise has taken place, we specifically build in silence as part of the debrief process so the subconscious can re-organize and rewrite old scripts based on the new insights. This burn-in or period of silence is an overlooked learning strategy that can provide real shifts if done well. Embrace the power of silence.

SECTION III:
The Details

Chapter 7:
Movement/Engagement

To really move them, move as you tell 'em

The moves you make will greatly affect the moods the audience will take. In most research done on public speaking effectiveness, **rapport is established and built in three ways:** 7% by words, 35% by tone of voice, and 58% by body language (especially the eyes).

However, body language can be interpreted in a positive or negative fashion. Here are the key positive and negative body language signals.

POSITIVE BODY LANGUAGE

- Direct eye contact. The eyes are seen as the window to the soul, so use them.
- Smiling. Smile often (when appropriate).
- Sitting squarely. Leaning slightly forward indicates you are paying attention.
- Nodding. Nodding in agreement is universally liked.
- A firm handshake.
- Calm. Presenting a calm exterior.
- Looking intently.

NEGATIVE BODY LANGUAGE

- Not looking at a person when speaking.
- Tapping a foot, finger, etc.
- Rocking backwards and forwards.
- Scratching. Picking at fingers or nails.
- Clearing your throat.
- Fiddling with hair, ear lobes, jewellery, jacket, glasses, etc.
- Nodding back and forth.
- Yawning.
- Looking at your watch or a clock.
- Standing too close. The "arms-length" rule is always recommended.
- Looking overly concerned. Considered falsely attentive.

Memorize these positive body language signals and you will project a better image and achieve an attentive audience.

GESTURES

Gestures can enhance or detract from your overall body language. So here are a few notes on proper gesturing.

- <u>Start with eye contact.</u> Being prepared! Having control of your message is a prerequisite for being able to project and establish a bond with the audience. Don't just pass your gaze throughout the room. Try to focus on individual listeners and create a bond with them by looking them directly in the eyes for 5 to 10 seconds.

- <u>Smile often!</u> Then do it some more.

- <u>Express emotion with your facial muscles.</u> For inspiration, check out *The Human Face*, a BBC documentary narrated by John Cleese of *Monty Python* fame.

- <u>Avoid distracting mannerisms.</u> Have a friend watch as you practice and look for nervous expressions such as fidgeting, twitching, lip biting, keys jangling, hands in pockets or behind the back.

- <u>Act like an actor telling a story.</u> Highlight the action verbs and look for ways to act out one or more parts. Things like running down the aisle and back if you are speaking about marathon running.

- <u>Don't copy gestures</u>. Avoid copying gestures from other speakers. Be you and respond naturally.

- <u>Make gestures convincing.</u> Every hand gesture should be total body movement that starts from the shoulder - never from the elbow. Half-hearted gestures look artificial.

- <u>Vary your speaking position.</u> Vary it by moving from one spot on the stage to another. Walk to the other side of the stage as you move to a new topic or move toward the audience as you ask a question.

POSITION VARIANCE

Change your body position. Zig Ziglar would often get down on one knee at the edge of the stage when he wanted to make a key point. He'd lower his whole body so he could be more eye level with his audience. This technique is a great attention grabber, a subtle signal indicator to anchor key points and can even be a "pattern interrupter" when used correctly *(explanation of "Pattern Interrupt" on page 44).*

OPEN THE ROOM

Do an experiment the next time you're in front of a group when someone is talking. When you ask a question and one of the participants is answering, get face to face with the person. Then do the opposite when another person is interacting with you by going to an opposite side of the room. As you do, watch the audience and be aware of the energy in the room. You will notice a difference.

Years ago, I was exposed to this concept of spatial positioning through accelerated learning and how this can work to cither bring your audience in or close them out. When you are in face-to-face close proximity for too long with a participant, it's as if you are having a one-on-one session, and effectively shuts out the group. If we open up the room by going to opposite sides or opposing corners, then we are keeping the rest of the group engaged and included in the exchange.

Periodically getting in a face-to-face position is not bad especially if you are together in front of the room for demos or role-plays.

The goal is to mix it up and change your spatial position to assist in the learning dynamics.

PHYSICAL CONNECTION

Roam the room and connect with people (if possible) before, during and after. If the group is small, make it a goal to talk to everyone before the program starts. This reduces resistance and creates an energetic connection—you with them and them with you.

Shake hands, high five or even do a soft fist bump to someone who did something great or made an insightful comment. Physically connecting is a form of celebrating success as well as forging a real bond with the audience. Be careful when doing this because of the vigilance regarding sexual harassment. Even this innocent act might be construed as unwanted and invasive. In some countries, unless you are well versed in the culture, it's best to leave it out. Shaking hands and looking a person in the eye for a job well done is accepted most everywhere.

STRATEGIES TO INSPIRE AND INFLUENCE DURING A SPEECH

One of the most important elements of doing presentations is the ability to inspire and influence people. Without these traits, even the most skilled team of seasoned professionals is unlikely to achieve great things. A highly inspired group of talented people, on the other hand, can move mountains. While it's true that inspiring people involves more than just changing the way you speak, there are some simple guidelines you can follow to help build influence with only your words and your voice.

Enthusiasm is contagious! Before you present your ideas, think about the aspects of the subject you find most interesting, and don't be afraid to let that interest come through in your voice.

Quotes, stories and anecdotes. Along with their obvious enter-tainment value, quotes and stories can lend authority to your topic and provide concrete examples people can relate to.

Confidence. Deliver your message loud and clear. Maintain eye contact with your listeners. Don't mumble or slouch.

You **and** *we,* **not** *I* **and** *me.* Instead of telling people what you want them to do, present ways for them to work together to achieve their goals. Involve listeners in the success of the group.

Simplicity. Keep it simple. People aren't motivated by what you say; they're motivated by what they understand. The best way to ensure audience understanding is to break down complex ideas into simple components.

Move around, gesture, motivate and make friends. No matter if it's a large or small group, connect with individual people through your eyes. How many times have you sat in a ballroom filled with thousands of people, and when the speaker connected with you through eye contact, you actually felt like he/she was speaking to only you? It makes people feel relevant.

Move to improve, motivate the mood, and engage from the stage with your use of the physical connection.

Chapter 8:
Problems/Mistakes

Problems and mistakes in telling 'em

- Hostile
- Critical
- Uninformed
- Sympathetic
- Monopolizer
- Shy Butterfly
- Private Conversation
- Free-For-All
- Argument
- Off the Subject

HANDLING PROBLEMS

AUDIENCES

Rarely will you ever have entire audiences of these different types, but you will frequently have one or more in an audience. Nonetheless, you must understand them and know how to work with them. An engaged audience may require persuasion. Some listeners will have different and not necessarily positive attitudes, and hence need special management and attention.

Here are four types of audiences (or individuals within an audience) and the problem behaviors they may exhibit:

Hostile

Open hostility is not uncommon to encounter in any of the three presentation types. It may be only from a few participants, but even one who reflects open disagreement with your message needs some special handling. They may not want to be there. They may be distracted. They may not like you. They may dislike what you say, mean or represent. The key is not allowing them to take over or distract from the intended outcome.

Here are some tips on handling hostility:

- Establish trust early.
- Find a way to agree with them.
- Address perceived disagreements early.
- Share alternate possibilities.
- Use reliable and not anecdotal evidence.

- Use acceptable and respected evidence and sources.
- Humor can help.
- Close with an undeniable conclusion.

Critical

Some audiences just think they are smarter than you, which could cause them to be critical of your offering. So prepare yourself.

- Back up your statements with verifiable evidence and good sources.
- Be careful with exaggeration and hyperbole.
- Employ common sense responses and avoid platitudes.
- Address both sides of an issue, good and bad, positive and negative.
- Respond with calm answers and even demeanor.

Uninformed

The uneducated, uninformed or just misinformed may argue or disagree.

- Ask relevant questions to find what and why they don't know something.
- Fill in details with indisputable facts.
- Logic is best to inform.
- See the lack of information as an opportunity to educate.

Sympathetic

Audiences who are sympathetic may not see the real issues because they are inclined to agree anyway.

- Challenge them.
- Make personal appeals, asking for their help.
- Trigger their feelings but don't overuse their built-in emotion.
- Be balanced in your viewpoint.

PEOPLE

Challenging workshop situations may arise during Speech, Facilitations and Training because of individuals rather than the whole audience. Some of them may occur during brief lectures or even team exercises. Here are some common problems encountered and tips for handling difficult situations and more importantly, difficult people.

The Monopolizer

This person typically uses more than his or her fair share of interaction time and tries to monopolize the discussion. Without discouraging them from contributing, you can handle the problem by avoiding eye contact and not calling on him or her, or by calling on him or her after everyone else has spoken (major points will have been made). If the person is particularly talkative, tactfully interrupt and ask a question of the group about a point the "Monopolizer" has made (in effect, "recapture" the discussion). This is a great place to use a "Pattern Interrupt" (see below explanation). Finally, if necessary, use the direct approach and interrupt by saying, *"Thank you. Let's see what some of your colleagues think."*

The Shy Butterfly

You can encourage individuals who are shy or hesitate to comment by asking them direct questions, and then following their comments with an encouraging statement like, *"What an interesting idea,"* or *"Thank you, Tom."*

Private Conversations

Ask the individuals to share their thoughts with the group, or simply give them silent eye contact until their attention is back on the group discussion. If you find these techniques a little manipulative, you can always use the direct approach and simply say, *"Could we please have everyone's attention? This, you won't want to miss."*

Free-For-All

This is a meeting facilitator's dream, since it shows real involvement. However, it also prevents the attendees from hearing everything so explain to the group that valuable ideas will be lost. Then ask an individual something like, *"John, what was it you were saying?"* as an orderly way to get the discussion going again.

Arguments

Differences of opinion are sure to occur during group discussions, and should be welcomed if they are brief and impersonal. If an argument develops and the participants become emotional, interrupt and explain 100% agreement isn't expected, and there are often two or more sides to an issue. In my experience, these differences of opinion are incredible learning opportunities if well facilitated and not allowed to get into dis-respect. People push back because they care, so I say let's positively harness the caring energy as a learning opportunity.

Off The Subject

The discussion should not be too tightly confined, but if it gets too involved with information irrelevant to the topic, simply say something like, *"Since we have a lot of material to cover today, let's get back to the original subject."*

PATTERN INTERRUPT

If the Facilitation or Training is going down a misguided path or someone specifically is trying to hijack the attention, then a "Pattern Interrupt" (PI) can be a subtle but highly effective way to bring the focus back on track.

TIP: Many times during a Training or facilitated session, I've had to use this because someone in the audience wants to overstay their time with the microphone or we've stumbled on an issue landmine that triggered pent-up negative emotion. In the right format, this emotion can be valuable. In the wrong format, this is a disaster and a recipe for losing the attention of the participants and the intended objectives.

Effective PIs, especially if someone is rambling, is to agree and/or acknowledge and weave into a question.

- *"I understand and let me ask the group a question."*
- *"I hear what you're saying, now let's consider_____."*
- *"Good point. Has anyone thought about _____?"*
- *"That is an interesting observation. Any other ideas from the room?"*

The goal is to subtly redirect the emotional current and direction of the point by causing a state of change. Some people think it's rude to interrupt. Here are two thoughts about that. First, if you get good at Pattern Interrupts, it is subtle and respectful. Second, if someone is rambling, others in the room want it to stop too, but it's not up to them to redirect the focus. The responsibility for the redirect belongs to the presenter. Mastering Pattern Interrupts is a highly valuable skill to keep the flow and energy moving in any group.

TALE: Tony Robbins was another of my early mentors. I attended many of Tony's programs and did several of the fire walk events he was noted for even before he had become a national and international force in the personal development industry. During one of Tony's extensive two-week training sessions, he taught us some very powerful communication techniques derived from Bandler and Grinder's work in NLP (Neuro Linguistic Programming). One of those NLP techniques is termed a Pattern Interrupt. Its purpose is:

A pattern interrupt can be employed to break a person's habit, state, or conversation. This is achieved by asking a question, saying something out of context or changing the person's mental environment. It is a sensory input that stops a pattern of behavior and leaves the person in an 'open' state.

After the completion of this two-week session with Tony, he indicated he was looking for a select group of people around the country to become "partners" in a venture to expand his new facilitated video training concept. Further, he challenged those who were interested to become "creative" in their attempts to get his attention for two reasons. First, he anticipated a large number of people would be vying for a limited number of positions. Second, he was looking only for the best people to be a part of this venture. So my business partner at the time came up with an idea to create a massive Pattern Interrupt to get Tony's attention. Key scene set: Even though we had been in several of Tony's programs recently, we assumed he would not remember us because we attended these sessions with hundreds of other people. As it turned out, we assumed right.

Tony was speaking two weeks later at the McCormick Center in Chicago in front of several thousand people. We decided to dress up in black suits reminiscent of the Blues Brothers look and got two wallets with children's sheriff badges pinned inside. We flew into Chicago the day of Tony's presentation and waited for him to take a break. During those days, Tony periodically stayed out front and answered questions from the audience during breaks. The minute the line of questioners finished, we walked up to Tony in our black suits and introduced ourselves in a very formal and stern voice, while simultaneously (and quickly) flashing our badges. We introduced ourselves as being from the IRS. Tony shook our hands and asked with great calmness, "What can I do for you?" I indicated we were there to speak with him about some "tax issues" and we would appreciate some time later today after his program to discuss these matters.

Up to this point, Tony was his typical cool and calm self but then his face went ashen. I knew we'd definitely interrupted his pattern and we needed to reveal the ploy immediately before this went any further. We introduced ourselves and recounted his challenge to get his attention and we wanted to come out to the castle in California and talk about this new partnership opportunity.

At that moment, I wasn't really sure if this 6'7" giant was going to hit us or hug us. He did neither but did give us the name of his assistant to set up the trip. We ended up going to California to discuss with Tony and his team the new venture but chose not to take action for a variety of reasons.

The lessons from this episode were numerous to include understanding the power of a Pattern Interrupt built around the letters I-R-S. In hindsight, I recognize this stunt may not have been well thought out due to the heart palpitations it could induce and the possible illegalities of representing oneself as a government agent even for one minute and 20 seconds.

The point of this story is to provide a setup for mastering the inherent power of the well-placed Pattern Interrupt.

MISTAKES
Mistakes while telling 'em

Screwing up is part of the process. So expect to mess up a few things but be ready to cure the problem. Here are some of the most common mistakes that will keep you from engaging your audience.

Biggest Mistakes:

- <u>Starting with a whimper</u>. Don't start with "Thank you for the kind introduction." Start with a bang! Give the audience a startling statistic, an interesting quote, a news headline, a question–something powerful that will get their attention immediately.

- <u>Attempting to imitate other speakers</u>. Authenticity is lost when you aren't yourself.

- <u>Failing to "work" the room</u>. Your audience wants to meet you. If you don't take time to mingle before the presentation, you lose an opportunity to enhance your credibility with your listeners.

- <u>Failing to use relaxation techniques</u>. Do whatever it takes– listening to music, breathing deeply, shrugging your shoulders–to relieve nervous tension. Use the EFT tapping technique covered in the Appendix.

- <u>Reading</u>. Reading a speech word for word. This will put the audience to sleep. Instead use a "keyword" outline: Look at the keyword to prompt your thoughts. Look into the eyes of the audience, and then speak.

- <u>Someone else's stories</u>. It's okay to use brief quotes from other sources, but to connect with the audience, you must illustrate your most profound thoughts from your own life experiences. If you think you don't have any interesting stories to tell, you are not looking hard enough.

- Speaking without passion. The more passionate you are about your topic, the more likely your audience will act on your suggestions.

- Ending a speech with questions and answers. Instead, tell the audience you will take questions and then say, "We will move to our closing point." After the Q and A, tell a story that ties in with your main theme, or summarize your key points. Conclude with a quote or call to action.

- Failing to prepare. Your reputation is at stake every time you face an audience, so rehearse well enough to ensure you'll leave a good impression!

- Failing to recognize speaking is an acquired skill. Effective professionals learn how to present in the same way they learn to use other tools to operate their businesses.

- Using the "words to die by": Refrain from constant use of aggravating words/phrases such as: **like, kinda, sorta, you know, um, uhhh**. Be careful how any of these phrases are used. They are passive, trite and annoy many people.

Chapter 9:
The Ending/The Exit/The Afterwards

Tell 'em what you told 'em

THE ENDING

So now we come to the end of your audience engagement. Here are the three primary fundamentals:

Summarize

Make sure you have summarized everything necessary in the presentation. Ask the rhetorical question and then answer for them: "What did we learn today?"

Energize

The finality of the engagement must be completed with energy. This is difficult mostly because you will be tired. But it will aid learning and bring the room's adrenalin level (not to mention blood sugar) up enough to want them to take action.

The Big Bang

Finish with a BANG! What you choose to say will be remembered, so choose it wisely.

POEM

My father was a great man in a multitude of ways. He was a community and business leader who really cared about people. He cared for his family, his community and especially the disadvantaged in ways that included giving years of his time and energy to make a lot of people's lives better. Upon his death, this poem was found on a piece of paper he carried in his wallet. I think it very clearly summed him up and I frequently <u>use it to powerfully close presentations</u>.

Class never runs scared. It is surefooted and confident. It can handle whatever comes along.

Class has a sense of humor. It knows that a good laugh is the best lubricant for oiling the machinery of human relations.

Class never makes excuses. It takes its lumps and learns from the past mistakes.

Class knows that good manners are nothing more than a series of petty sacrifices.

Class bespeaks an aristocracy that has nothing to do with money. Some extremely wealthy people have no class at all while others who are struggling to make ends meet are loaded with it.

Class is real. You can't fake it.

The person with class makes everyone feel comfortable because he is comfortable with himself.

If you have class, you've got it made. If you don't have class, no matter what else you have, it doesn't make any difference.

THE EXIT

Telling 'em after it's over

So now you've ended with a bang. A great opportunity presents itself to:

1. Get more business;
2. Answer specific questions;
3. Sell your message; or
4. Just connect with people for a possible next level win/win relationship.

As the majority of people file out, a few will approach you. Make sure you stay around to visit.

Do these things at the EXIT:

Talk to people afterwards
If you have engaged the audience, you will have a great opportunity to personally connect with people who approach you because, well frankly, you did your job well. Congratulations! So talk to them. Answer their questions. Make a connection. But keep the interactions to 2-3 minutes if others are waiting.

Pass out information, cards or swag
Some shy people may only want to meet and thank you. Do so graciously and give them something. They will be honored by the gesture, and will use that validation to remember you again, and maybe benefit the cause of further engaging another audience.

Exchange ideas

Ask questions of those people who took time to approach you.

"What did you like best about the training?"

"Are you likely to attend another presentation if I do one?"

"Was there anything I could have done differently to better meet your needs?"

People love to be asked their opinions by a presenter. It is an honor and a show of respect. You will almost always get a piece of information you might not ordinarily receive.

Making One-on-One follow-up plans

Use the moment to plan specific contact in the future. The audience member obviously approached you for a reason. So use the opportunity to make definitive lunch, dinner, meeting, conference call plans or just an email exchange. It's easier than you think.

THE AFTER

Remind them later what you told 'em

In the aftermath of the presentation, follow up with the attendees. It could be via a blog post, social media or just a newsletter sent.

Follow-up Methods

Review any evaluation forms completed. People will generally be honest when they can fill out these forms anonymously. There is a treasure trove of feedback in the words. So review them carefully, because you will read things that might make you uncomfortable...and better.

Encourage

Based on different personality styles, some people may seem a bit standoffish to you in person but more confident if you ask them to contact you by email or otherwise. Encourage them to contact you with further follow-up questions or just information they want to impart.

Remind

After a few days have passed, you can reinforce individual learning by sending a summary of key points to all audience members. This can be done through blogs, social media or emails.

Motivate

Encourage and motivate the participants to contact you. Offer a free evaluation of something they had questions about, or offer a free item to the first 10 followers on Twitter. There will be much more effective follow-up if the audience is incentivized to do so.

TO SIMPLIFY AND MAXIMIZE "THE AFTER"

For those who use speaking, training and facilitation as simultaneous opportunities to bring value to clients and increase your visibility in the marketplace, you will need an effective way to keep in touch with customers, attendees and prospects alike. After many years of searching, I found a top-notch business and marketing platform to handle contact management, payment processing, automated marketing and affiliate management.

Ontraport is an all-in-one business and marketing system to free you up from the burden of detailed operational tasks so you can focus on your clients and do more of the things you love to build your business.

To learn more about Ontraport go to: http://goo.gl/vyKqDK

Ontraport

CONCLUSION

MY WANT FOR YOU

The original goal for this book was to capture over 30 years of experiences to help you achieve presentation mastery faster, better and easier and with less fear all while having more fun, influence and prosperity. Further, it has been my intention to help people break through the blocks that keep their message stifled no matter how introverted, extroverted, young or old, experienced or inexperienced. In addition, to help give a commanding voice to those who have something of value to share with the other seven billion on the planet.

There's an energetic shift taking place in the world; and vital to ushering in these changes, I believe more individuals will be compelled to speak authentically about what's in their head, heart and soul. As people work through their fears/blocks, move into the growth stage by teaching what they most need to learn, reach mastery then naturally elevate toward the betterment of those around them, a transformative shift cannot help but take place.

If you have something powerful inside of you to share and have been stopped based on an outdated mental script about presenting in public, know that there are highly effective ways to get through the blocks (See EFT, RAMP AND CORE MAP).

FEAR AND "EDU-TRAIN-MENT™"

Speeches, Facilitations and Training. They all differ but are interwoven with each other. In order to "Totally Engage Your Audience," you must *educate* them, you must *train* them, and you must *entertain* them. **"Edu-Train-Ment™."** The "Edu-Train-Ment™" concept emphasizes the importance of understanding these ideas and their value in conquering your fears, speaking with authority, presenting with authenticity and being successful at any of these presentation types.

I hope this book has been "EDU-TRAIN-MENT™" for you and proven beneficial in helping you learn to engage an audience through effective Speeches, Facilitations and Training. It is also my sincere hope this book has opened you up to the reality that fear need not stop you from doing anything you want to, including speaking in front of others. Remember the three fears of ridicule, rejection and embarrassment? Well, you now have three proven processes (EFT, RAMP and CORE MAP) to get you through those old beliefs that have blocked you from getting what you desire. You need not fear again!

NEVER GIVE UP BEING YOU...

...even for an instant. Consistently honor your own natural style. The minute you give up who you are is the minute you start losing the audience. The greatest personal gift from these years of experience came in the form of self-confidence so I could finally give myself permission to be authentically who I am in front of any group. Authenticity is engagement.

Once you find the authentic you, then it's time to go about the engagement of any audience in a fearless way and ultimately creating the life you desire

For more information on group programs or how CORE MAP and RAMP can cause you to move toward your goals faster, better and easier, contact:

Marc Schwartz
Email: marc@energyofsuccess.net
Visit our website at: **www.energyofsuccess.net**

Energy of Success

APPENDIX

Learn about proven and powerful processes that will move you past any emotional block you are dealing with...to include those mental barriers that keep you from comfortably speaking in front of others.

SUCCESS IS JUST AROUND THE BLOCK

"Surveys show that the #1 fear of Americans is public speaking. #2 is death. That means that at a funeral, the average American would rather be in the casket than doing the eulogy."

Jerry Seinfeld

Have you ever been overlooked or disregarded for an opportunity, job, or experience that you wanted because you were not confident in your ability to speak in front of others? Have you ever played small and not gone after something you desired because you did not want to put yourself in an embarrassing situation that might involve speaking in front of others? Has it ever crossed your mind that even though you have great insight, skills, mastery and capabilities on a certain subject, you fly under the radar and rebuff all opportunities to speak to others on a topic you are passionate about because you do not have confidence in your ability to talk in a group setting?

When Would Now Be A Good Time To Change This Old, Non-Productive Pattern?

Please get really clear that you were not born with these fears about speaking in front of others. These mental blocks, fears and barriers are not really yours; they're all made up. They are conditioned responses. We learned them and embodied them as real through some catalyzing event(s) earlier in our lives when we did not have the tools or insights to be aware of them, let alone change them. Worse yet is when we have the skills and knowledge of a particular topic and, because of this historical conditioning, we continue to waste valuable time fighting the little voice inside us that questions whether or not we can actually DO this. It is persistent, unending, debilitating and damn frustrating.

In Chapter 1, I explained RAMP (Rapid Accelerated Mind Patterning) and EFT (Emotional Freedom Technique), two powerful processes to help you overcome that consistent little voice, which can and will stop forward progress. Now I want to share some additional energy psychology strategies that <u>will</u> move you past the blocks that are stopping you. I do so because identifying and getting past these blocks will allow you to envision your future more clearly. It will allow you to move closer and closer to being that master presenter you desire to be and do so in a faster, better and easier approach than relying on your own strained attempts at pure willpower which is a short-term fix at best.

Contained in this added Appendix is a list of proven strategies and techniques to help you get past your internal blocks. I do a deeper review on the processes that I've had experience with and believe to be the most efficacious and at the very least provide overviews and websites for the remainder. If you incorporate even a few of these techniques into your developmental process, you'll find that you're not only more prepared, but also more self-confident. You'll be on your way to fulfilling your dreams and know, for sure, that *Success Is Just Around The Block* for you.

The Laws of Energy and The Subconscious Mind

Let's set the stage by understanding more about two of the most powerful forces in the universe – the irrefutable laws of energy (physics) and the very specific rules of the subconscious mind. Understanding how these two forces work individually and in combination can provide predictable, repeatable, quantum leaps in human achievement, including speaking and presenting in front of others.

If you really want to move forward, then it's time to increase your awareness of how these two forces – the laws of energy and the subconscious mind – can form the basis for transforming your life. Such an awareness is a major step toward connecting with your authentic self, as well as with any audience you choose, to reach the levels of mastery you desire - not just in speaking and presenting, but in any aspect of life.

ENERGY MODEL AND THE 24
UNBREAKABLE RULES OF THE SUBCONSCIOUS

If everything in this world is energy (which it is), it stands to reason that everything, including humans, must obey the laws that govern energy. If we fully understand the laws of energy and how energy works, we can more effectively apply this understanding to individuals, as well as to families, groups, teams, companies and even countries, to know why things are or are not working.

The key is **awareness**. We must understand and be **aware** that the irrefutable laws of energy are predictable and repeatable. When we understand and are purposeful about directing that energy, we can have quantum movement at any level of human accomplishment, including that of being a truly masterful presenter.

Taking this one step further, we must agree that thoughts are energy - that all physical reality is made up of vibrations of energy - and that even our thoughts are vibrations of energy. This is the new reality that quantum physics has revealed to us. Our thoughts have a powerful influence on how we create our lives.

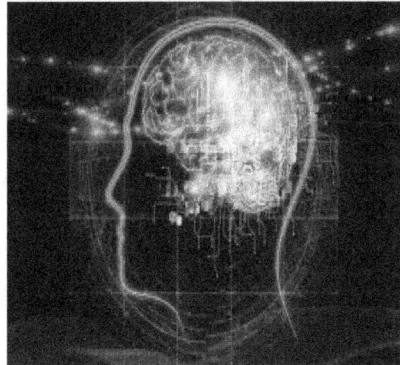

"Thoughts are energy, the same as everything else. The higher the frequency of our thought/brain wave, the higher the consciousness" (Baska).

"A fundamental conclusion of the new physics also acknowledges that the observer creates the reality. As observers, we are personally involved with the creation of our own reality" (Henry).

To better understand how to create and manifest the life we desire, we must appreciate how our subconscious mind works in concert with these laws of energy. At a very basic level, you must be aware that the rules the subconscious mind follows are completely different from the rules of the conscious mind. In addition to the subconscious mind working for your benefit 100% of the time and being thousands of times more powerful than the conscious mind, there are twenty-four identified, unbreakable rules for the subconscious that we must follow if we want to be successful in reaching any outcome.

The first eight of these rules come from the works of psychiatrist/psychologist Milton H. Erickson and hypnotherapist Charles Tebbetts. Rules Nine through Fifteen were added based on the work done by Richard Bandler and John Grinder on Neuro-Linguistic Programming (NLP).

Later, after more than 20 years of researching subconscious processes and working with people at the subconscious level, Dr. Sherry Buffington, an internationally known author, presenter, consultant, trainer and coach, as well as the president and CEO of Quantum Leap Systems, Inc., identified Rules Sixteen through Twenty-four. It is with much thanks to Dr. Buffington's research that we can now understand how the subconscious works and use that understanding to help create the lives we choose.

THE SUBCONSCIOUS MIND BUILDS STORIES

Dr. Buffington's research shows us that the conscious mind is logical, while the subconscious is "imaginal." While our conscious minds use *reason*, our subconscious minds rely on *images*. And within this "imaginal" subconscious, we build stories. Whether the stories are based in fact is not important. The stories only need to be conceptually believable. Our conscious mind searches out information and sends it to our subconscious mind, which, in turn, takes it in, translates it into a complete story and figures out where to store it. According to Buffington, it's important to remember that the subconscious is not concerned with logic. Logic and reason are left for the conscious mind to deal with. Once the conscious mind has passed this information on to the subconscious, it goes in search of more information. It is when reasoning and the imagination (the conscious and subconscious minds) conflict that problems surface. And when such conflicts do arise, the imagination - the subconscious- wins.

Buffington goes on to reason that, although sometimes it might seem that we can, we cannot consciously *will* our way to making changes or eliminating fear. That is because logic and reasoning are employed by the conscious mind, but neither of these two conscious efforts affect the subconscious. Trying to enlist a logical path of action cannot work until you *imagine* yourself doing whatever it is you want or need to do.

So if we take Buffington's words to heart, it becomes apparent that if someone desires to be a fearless and powerful presenter, then most, if not all, the changes he or she needs to make for different outcomes are changes that are mental or imaginal.

Buffington goes on to suggest that as long as we resist change, we cannot change. When we refuse to let go of our present view of reality, we are, in effect, resisting our own efforts to get things right – which leaves us stuck. Before we can change the reality in which we exist – before we can change a bad habit or unappealing physical condition – we must change how we view the world. "The subconscious mind is like a homing device," Buffington notes. "It unfailingly follows whatever we focus on. Time and time again, it returns to the ideas (the reality) of which we take ownership" (Buffington, *Banish Blocks)*.

She also shares the research of Napoleon Hill in his well-known book entitled *Think and Grow Rich*. Hill spent thirty years tracking successful men and eventually came to a singular conclusion. Those who are successful achieve success because they very clearly see (visualize) what it is that they want. Because they have such a clear, visual *image* of their success, they can confidently *own* that success.

The trouble, Buffington goes on to say, is all of the "stuff" we allow to get in our way: "Clarity and ownership are the ultimate keys to success. But here's the rub: Until you get all the old rubbish cluttering your mind out of your way, you have no choice but to deal with it. And as long as you're dealing with all that "stuff," you are stuck where you are." (Buffington, *Banish Blocks*).

"Research shows that more than 95% of what prevents us from moving forward boldly and realizing our dreams is nonphysical. In other words, it's all in our minds…"
Dr. Sherry Buffington
https://banishblocks.com

According to Dr. Buffington, as the smallest of babies, we have but one fear, and that is the fear of the unknown. What we have come to fear as adults has all been developed through our conditioning. She argues that some of these developed fears are, of course, helpful. Because we have fear, we can avoid things that might hurt us. However, most of our fears are far from helpful. If we are afraid to think about getting up and walking across a room or of speaking with someone we don't know or of soliciting clients to purchase what we know will be good for them, then fear is certainly not beneficial. Instead, it has gotten in our way.

It is these fears gone amiss that have resulted in the blocks and barriers keeping us from success. "Perhaps," she says, "these fear-induced stumbling blocks worked for us when we were children. Unfortunately for so many of us, they simply do not work for us now."

According to Buffington, there are only four things keeping us from realizing our dreams:

1. Fear (about 60% of the cause)
2. Erroneous beliefs (about 25% of the cause)
3. Lack of knowledge (about 10% of the cause)
4. Physical barriers (about 5% of the cause)

She believes that it is our fear and/or our inaccurate beliefs about what we can and cannot do, which have thwarted us in learning whatever it is we need to learn to move forward in overcoming our mental blocks and barriers. And, that, in turn, means that the only thing stopping us from having what we want (all but a mere 5%, which are the actual physical barriers to our success) is not real. It is imagined.

Buffington shares the example of a blind man wanting nothing more than to fly a commercial plane or one who has lost the use of his limbs dreaming of dancing in the ballet. These individuals, sadly, must confront legitimate physical barriers. For most of us, thankfully, our real physical impediments are few. We've all read the stories of those brave men and women who have overcome their actual physical limitations to perform amazing feats of strength and endurance. "If just one person has overcome what we perceive to be a limitation," Buffington states, "we cannot honestly consider it a legitimate physical limitation at all." (Buffington, *Banish Blocks*).

As we continue to strive toward becoming the master presenters we know we can be, it is helpful to understand Dr. Buffington's insights into how we can overcome our perceived limitations.

Three of Dr. Sherry Buffington's "24 Unbreakable Rules of the Subconscious Mind":

1. Every thought or idea causes a physiological reaction.

> The subconscious mind rules your emotions. It can make you feel happy, or it can make you feel sad. It can increase your energy and motivate you, or it can suppress your energy and keep you depressed and miserable.

> And because emotions directly affect your physical functioning, your subconscious mind can make you sick or keep you well. Thoughts filled with strong emotional content always reach the subconscious mind and make an impression. Once accepted into the subconscious mind, these thoughts generate ideas, and the ideas continue to produce the same physical reactions over and over again. When these reactions are not pleasing or beneficial, conflict arises in the form of mental, emotional and/or physical anguish. In order to eliminate or change our chronic, negative reactions, we must connect with the subconscious mind and change the patterns responsible for these negative reactions.

2. *Imagination is more powerful than knowledge.*

This is an important rule to remember. Any thought or idea accompanied by a strong emotion, such as anger, hatred, love or political or religious beliefs, *cannot be modified through the use of reason.* Have you ever tried to reason with people who hold a strong belief? You typically cannot, no matter how crazy the belief might be or how much logical evidence you produce to disprove it.

3. *Once a belief or idea has been accepted by the subconscious mind, it remains until it is replaced by another belief or idea.*

The longer a belief is held, the more it tends to become a fixed thought pattern. This is how habits of action are formed, both good and bad.

(Note: Information on the "24 Unbreakable Rules of the Subconscious Mind" comes from Dr. Sherry Buffington's *Banish Blocks:* https://banishblocks.com).

Get The FREE 24 Unbreakable Rules of the Subconscious Mind Full Report at https://energyofsuccess.net/members/

24 Rules

You can see how important it is to understand the workings of the conscious and subconscious minds if you are to achieve success fully. As you work toward overcoming the mental blocks and barriers keeping you from your dream of becoming the master of your own reality, you can also benefit from the insights of acclaimed speaker, best-selling author and Olympic speed skier Vince Poscente, who understands the importance of resiliency in overcoming challenges.

In his book *The Ant and the Elephant*, Poscente compares the powerful relationship between the conscious and subconscious minds to that of an ant and an elephant. (He shared his thoughts on this process in a recent Energy of Success Podcast: http://bit.ly/2pmhlVp).

THE STORY OF *THE ANT AND THE ELEPHANT*

"I want to add something about a book I wrote called *The Ant and the Elephant*. *The Ant and the Elephant* is a parable about an ant trying to get to an oasis. The ant engages an elephant to help him get there.

"The size differential between the ant and elephant is similar to the difference between the powers of the conscious and subconscious minds. This information comes from Dr. Lee Pulos and is a way to metaphorically note the distinct capacity differences and processing capabilities between the two distinct parts of the brain."

"In a second of time, your conscious mind is processing with 2,000 neurons. In the same second, your subconscious mind is processing with 4 billion neurons. Two thousand conscious neurons versus 4 billion subconscious neurons....so who's in control? Obviously, the subconscious mind is in control. But we have never really understood that. It's been the grand illusion. We wander around through life thinking that 'we' (our conscious minds) are in control. However, we don't know what we don't know because it is really the massive subconscious mind that is acting out its agenda."

"Imagine what could happen if you were the architect of that agenda? What if you were the architect of your subconscious direction? How powerful would your life and your actions be if the 2,000 neurons of your conscious mind and the 4 billion neurons of your subconscious mind were all headed in the exact same direction? How much easier would things be?" (Poscente, Episode 5: Becoming the Architect of Your Subconscious: available at http://bit.ly/2pmhlVp).

(Note: You can find *The Ant and the Elephant: Leadership for the Self: A Parable and 5-Step Action Plan to Transform Workplace Performance* at: http://amzn.to/2rA0NON).

IF THIS ISSUE OF BLOCKS AND BARRIERS ISN'T SETTLED QUICKLY, IT MAY LAST A WHILE.
Almost anything is possible if we can just get the blocks out of our way. Imagine what you could achieve if you could eliminate the internal blocks that keep you stuck. Imagine if you could stop doing the things that are keeping you unhealthy, damaging your relationships, diminishing your joy or keeping you from realizing your dreams.

If your dream is to be in front of an audience as much as possible and use your natural power to stir them to something greater but you remain locked into the mental scripts that keep you from moving toward these goals, then let me help. I've spent tens of thousands of dollars and thousands of hours looking for every possible way to overcome these barriers faster, easier and better. Now, with these processes, it is possible to remove these blocks and barriers quickly and, in several cases, for good.

Energy Psychology Strategies to Get You Past Your Blocks:

* RAMP (www.banishblocks.com)

- Logosynthesis (http://logosynthesiscolorado.com/)
- TAT – Tapas Accupressure Technique (www.tatlife.com)
- EFT – Emotional Freedom Technique
  (http://www.emofree.com/)
  (http://www.thetappingsolution.com/)
- Power Phrase Technique (http://myinnermastery.com)
- EMDR – Eye Movement Desensitization & Reprocessing
  (http://www.emdr.com/what-is-emdr/) and Robert An-
  drews, M.A., founder and director of The Institute of
  Sports Performance (www.tinssp.com)
- The Sedona Method (http://www.sedona.com/home.asp)
- NLP – Neuro-Linguistic Programming
  (http://www.nlplearningsystems.com/index.htm)
- Psych-K (https://www.psych-k.com/)
- Hypnosis
- Behavioral Kinesiology

RAMP (Rapid Accelerated Mind Patterning)

RAMP, which I introduced earlier, is a powerful, safe and simple technique for instantly and permanently transforming old, ineffective programs into beneficial new ones and for rapidly removing blocks to success. RAMP works by simply having a conversation with the subconscious mind, using its own language and rules, so that subconscious patterns are updated and perfectly aligned with conscious desires. RAMP is effective for removing unwanted behaviors and feelings, the effects of trauma, grief, anxiety and depression and fears and phobias of all kinds. It is also effective for reducing chronic pain and eliminating many psychosomatic and stress-based symptoms (such as migraines and other types of headaches and back pain caused by over-stressed muscles) and for eliminating bad habits.

Because the RAMP method uses an individual's own subconscious processes, it is exceptionally effective (the success rate is better than 97%) and *completely* safe. The subconscious mind allows only changes it perceives as beneficial, so it is not possible to create conditions that are harmful. (To learn more about RAMP, visit: https://energyofsuccess.net/processes/).

RAMP

LOGOSYNTHESIS

Created by Swiss psychologist Dr. Willem Lammers, Logosynthesis is a guided, self-change technique. Since 2005, this strategy has been used by psychotherapists and coaches throughout Europe to help their clients eliminate stress, worry and anxiety. The process, as explained by internationally known psychotherapist, counselor and life coach Dr. Laurie Weiss, is simple and involves only a couple of minutes a day to release the energy that is stuck and causing stress.

Negative Mental Stories (triggers) Freeze Energy
It's completely natural to create negative mental stories in reaction to our fears. The trouble with these stories is twofold. First, the stories cause us even more unnecessary stress, worry and anxiety. Secondly, and unfortunately, we believe these stories to be true and they become "triggers." We react to these made-up stories as if they were a source of present danger.

Top 10 Reasons We Make Up Stories:

1. The presence of an event from the past we were unable to cope with, which our brains have stored as pictures, sounds and/or a sensations

2. Replaying a memory of this event
3. Encountering something in the present that reawakens the memory of this event
4. A current event that strains our resources, especially if it reminds us of past, stressful events
5. A current event that doesn't match our beliefs about ourselves, others, or the world
6. Anticipating that the future will be uncomfortable or unpleasant – such as not having enough money
7. Being reminded of the experience of a trauma that once overwhelmed our resources – we may or may not remember it
8. Trying to solve an impossible problem – such as getting a dead person to change how he or she treated you when he or she was alive
9. Imagining that something that happened in the past is going to happen again in the future – such as being in an automobile accident
10. Anticipating breaking rules you learned as a child

Answering the following questions will give you clues to the stories (triggers) you use to keep your system in a state of arousal and/or a state of stress, anxiety, or worry.

- What can't I stop thinking about?
- What do I avoid because it scares me or because I feel as if I can't stand it?
- What did I experience (think, feel, notice) just before experiencing discomfort?
- Was this real or imagined?

Using words as tools, Logosynthesis will help you release the negative energy stored in these stories/triggers. It will help you reclaim your positive energy to use in any way you choose.

Logosynthesis uses three important sentences of correction (listed below). As you say the sentences aloud, keep in mind the following:

- The "I" in each sentence refers to your Essence – the part of you that is an expression of all that is "you" – your Higher Self – your True Self – what some call Your Soul.

- A brief statement of your "trigger" goes in the brackets in each sentence. Your trigger is a memory, fantasy or belief that is related to your frozen energy and is causing you distress. It is whatever you can't get out of your mind – whatever makes you crazy, distracts you or keeps you from connecting to your Essence. For example, your trigger statement might be "If I do this, I will fail."

- Say each sentence out loud; pause between the sentences and notice what thoughts, feelings, images, etc., come to you. Don't try to understand the meaning of the sentences; just let the words work.

Sentences of Correction:

1. I retrieve all of my energy bound up in [insert Trigger Statement] and return it to the right place in my Self.
2. I remove all the non-me energy related to [insert Trigger Statement] from all of my cells, from my body and from my personal space and send it to where it truly belongs.
3. I retrieve all my energy bound up in all my reactions to [insert Trigger Statement] and take it back to the right place in my Self.

Once you feel that your energy has shifted toward more positive feelings, say:

4. I tune all of my systems to this new awareness.

Use this process as often as you like for any different triggers you discover.

(The information on Logosynthesis comes from Dr. Laurie Weiss. To get her book *Letting it Go: Relieve Anxiety and Toxic Stress in Just a Few Minutes Using Only Words*, go to: http://amzn.to/2khA1XM).

TAT (Tapas Acupressure Technique)

TAT® is a process developed by Tapas Fleming, a Licensed Acupuncturist in California, which focuses the user on a series of statements while holding acupressure points that connect all physical, mental, emotional and spiritual parts. While in the TAT® pose, you can free the parts of you that are stuck in a trauma, negative belief or physical disease through focusing on specific statements, which are the "Steps of TAT®" The TAT® process enables your entire system – physical, mental, emotional and spiritual – to be present in the current moment and more able to receive the love, healing, peace and energy available to you now. TAT® has been used successfully to end fears and phobias, lessen every kind of stress – both past and current – and heal the emotional origins of physical disease.

The TAT® process begins with a statement of intention and includes several steps described below: (To learn more, go to: http://www.tatlife.com/).

The Intention
The healing I am about to do is on behalf all of my ancestors, my family, everyone involved, all parts of myself, all points of view I have ever held and anyone else who would like to benefit from this healing.

The Problem - *(Step 1)*
This happened.

The Opposite of the Problem - *(Step 2)*
This happened. It's over. I'm okay and I can relax now.

The Places - *(Step 3)*
All the places in my mind, body and life where this has been stored are healing now, *or* God, thank you for healing all the places in my mind, body and life where this has been stored.

(You do not need to know what all the places are; just make the intention that they're healing now.)

The Origins - *(Step 4)*
All the origins of this are healing now, *or* God, thank you for healing all the origins of this.

(You do not need to know what all the origins are; just make the intention that they're healing now.)

Forgiveness - *(Step 5)*
All the communications and connections related to this are completing now. I apologize to everyone I hurt related to this and wish them love, happiness and peace, *or* I forgive everyone who hurt me related to this and wish them love, happiness and peace. I forgive everyone I blamed for this, including God and myself.

(It is not necessary to think of each person involved; just make the intention of forgiveness with your heart.)

Healing - *(Step 6)*
All the parts of me that were affected from this are healing now.

Whatever's Left - *(Step 7)*
Whatever's left over concerning this issue can heal now.

(Review the original problem to see if there is any aspect that still has a negative emotional charge for you. If there is something left, do TAT about whatever it is before proceeding.)

Choosing - *(Step 8)*
I choose (whatever positive outcome you want related to this).

Integration - *(Step 9)*
This healing is now completely integrated with my grateful thanks, *or* God, thank you for completely integrating this healing now.

Of course, the real test for how effective TAT is will be the changes you see in your life. With some sessions, you may feel immediate, big shifts – a weight that suddenly lifts from your shoulders and/or a dramatic easing of pain or tension. Other times, the changes might be much more subtle. One day you may realize that you simply haven't thought about the problem for weeks, even though it used to be on your mind every day. You may find yourself in the midst of doing something you would never have dreamed possible but are now doing easily without a second thought. All of these changes contribute to your living a happier life.

EFT (Emotional Freedom Technique)

The Emotional Freedom Technique (EFT) is a form of psychological acupressure based on the same energy meridians (channels) used for over five thousand years in traditional acupuncture to treat physical and emotional ailments, but without the invasiveness of needles.

EFT is based on the discovery that imbalances in the body's energy system have profound effects on one's personal psychology. Correcting these imbalances, which is done by tapping on certain body locations, often leads to rapid reduction in stress. And by rapid, I mean **stress can vanish in minutes!!!**

EFT focuses on the body's subtle energy meridians. Simply stated, it is an emotional version of acupuncture, but needles aren't necessary. Instead, you stimulate well-established energy meridian points on your body by tapping on them with your fingertips.

Use EFT prior to any program you're presenting, especially if you're feeling stress. It's a simple and fast way to let go of stress and to be present and focused on the audience.

"THE CAUSE OF NEGATIVE EMOTIONS IS A DISRUPTION IN THE BODY'S ENERGY SYSTEM."
GARY CRAIG, EFT CREATOR

In this technique, tapping on designated points on the face and body is combined with verbalizing the identified problem and followed by a general affirmation phrase. Combining these ingredients of the EFT technique balances the energy system and relieves psychological stress and psychological pain.

Each EFT tapping exercise consists of a **SETUP** statement, followed by two rounds of tapping a sequence of **8 EFT** body points. **ROUND 1** focuses on the problem by repeating the *negative reminder phrase,* while **ROUND 2** focuses on the solution by verbalizing *preferences, choices and possible alternate outcomes.*

SEQUENCE OF TAPPING POINTS
1. Eyebrow
2. Side of Eye
3. Under Eye

4. Under Nose

5. Chin

6. Collarbone

7. Under Arm

8. Top of Head

SETUP STATEMENT

- Rate intensity of the issue being addressed on a scale of 0-10:
    - 10 = strong discomfort
    - 0 = no discomfort

Tap the karate chop point on either side of your hand continuously while repeating the entire set-up statement for the issue being addressed 3 times.

Example of a SETUP Statement:
"Even though I have this fear that people will reject me if I present in front of a group, I'm learning to deeply and completely accept myself."

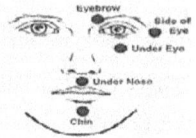

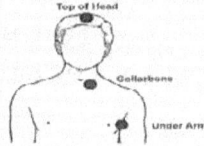

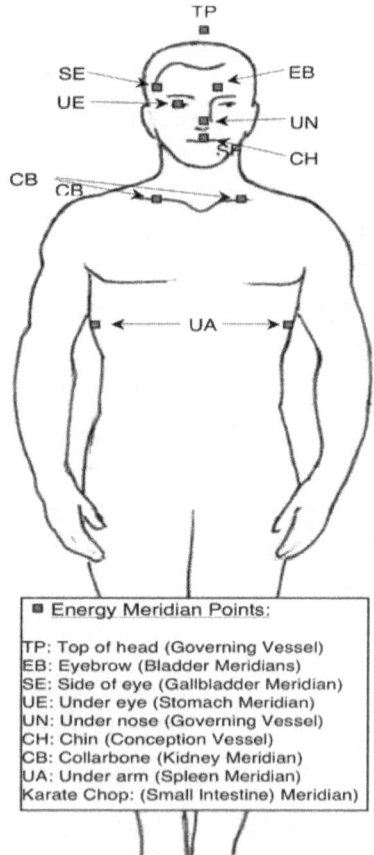

☐ Energy Meridian Points:

TP: Top of head (Governing Vessel)
EB: Eyebrow (Bladder Meridians)
SE: Side of eye (Gallbladder Meridian)
UE: Under eye (Stomach Meridian)
UN: Under nose (Governing Vessel)
CH: Chin (Conception Vessel)
CB: Collarbone (Kidney Meridian)
UA: Under arm (Spleen Meridian)
Karate Chop: (Small Intestine) Meridian)

NEGATIVE TAPPING SEQUENCE

Starting at the eyebrow point, begin tapping each point in the sequence of points approximately 7-10 times while repeating the negative reminder phrase.

Example of a Negative
Reminder Phrase:
"I am afraid people will reject me if I present in front of them."

POSITIVE TAPPING SEQUENCE

Starting at the eyebrow point again, tap each point 7-10 times while repeating the sequence of **8 positive phrases**.

This allows you to install what you would prefer to experience emotionally in your thought patterns and in your life.

Example of 8 Positive Phrases:
- Eyebrow – I feel acceptable now.
- Side of Eye – I accept success.
- Under Eye – I release the need for other people's approval.
- Under Nose – I appreciate who I am.
- Chin – I feel acceptable inside.
- Collarbone – I accept success no matter what others think.
- Under Arm – I open all channels for success.
- Top of Head – I appreciate how worthy I am.

DEEP BREATH

Take a slow, deep breath to move the energy through your body and further anchor your preferred thought patterns.

Understand that fear is a necessary, unavoidable and natural biological response to a new situation. Fear helps us survive difficult situations. Fear is an early warning system that protects us, but fear also announces something that might surprise you. It says,

"Hey, opportunity is knocking. Answer the door." It's time to banish your fear and embrace your courage so that you can open the door to opportunity.

POWER PHRASE TECHNIQE

Another powerful option is the Power Phrase Technique from Mark Youngblood's new book, *Dear Human, Master Your Emotions.* The goal is to anchor a "power phrase" to moments in your life when you felt safe, powerful and successful.

The first step is to come up with a power phrase to say to yourself as you are about to go on for your speech. Have fun creating the strongest, most meaningful power phrase you can:

> "I'm going to nail this!"
> "They're going to love me!"
> "I'm going to rock this place!"
> "I am powerful!"
> "This is my time to shine!"
> "I can do this!"

Now, you want to "anchor" the supportive feeling states like feeling successful, confident, powerful, and having fun to your power phrase. By doing so, you will *anchor* the states of success (you *can* do this), of confidence (you *have* achieved), and of power (you *do* have the inner strength to take on this challenge).

Complete the following process for each of the feeling states, each time using the same power phrase and finger combination (which I'll describe below) so you can "load" the feeling states into the power phrase.

1. Close your eyes.

2. Recall a time when you felt the positive feeling state. Let's use confidence as an example. It doesn't matter what you felt confident about, just that it was something you had to master and now have complete confidence in being able to do (lifting a heavy weight, cooking a complicated dish, taking a great photograph, making your children laugh, etc.).

3. The key is to put yourself back into the original event as if it were happening. Vividly see, hear and feel yourself confidently completing the action. Amplify your feelings of confidence about being able to do this. At the peak intensity of these feelings, start repeating your power phrase in your mind, such as "I can do this!" At the same time, bend your "pinkie" finger down and place your thumb over the nail to hold it in the bent position. Use your non-dominant hand. (This simultaneously sets a physical anchor.)

4. Continue this for 10-20 seconds to fully anchor these powerful positive feelings.

5. Repeat this process for each of the other positive feeling states you want to add to your power phrase.

Then, just before you step up to do your speech, start saying your power phrase using the same finger position from the anchoring process to fire the anchor. You will be flooded with those positive feelings.

(Note: To get Mark Youngblood's book, go to:
http://MasterYourEmotionsBook.com)

EMDR

EMDR (Eye Movement Desensitization and Reprocessing) is a psychotherapy that enables people to heal from the symptoms and emotional distress that are the result of disturbing life experiences. EMDR therapy shows that the mind can, in fact, heal from psychological trauma, much as the body recovers from physical trauma. When you cut your hand, your body works to close the wound. If a foreign object or repeated injury irritates the wound, it festers and causes pain. Once the foreign object or repeated injuries that obstruct healing are removed, healing resumes. EMDR therapy demonstrates that a similar sequence of events occurs with mental processes. The brain's information processing system naturally moves toward mental health. If the system is blocked or imbalanced by the impact of a disturbing event, the emotional wound festers and can cause intense suffering. Once the block is removed, healing resumes.

SEDONA METHOD

The Sedona Method is a process that helps you to change yourself from the inside out by showing you how to eliminate the unconscious blocks that hold you back from having, being and doing what you choose. There are three ways to approach the process of releasing mental blocks, and they all lead to the same result: a liberating of your natural ability to let go of any unwanted emotion on the spot and an allowing of the suppressed energy in your subconscious to dissipate. The first way to release your mental blocks is by choosing to let go of the unwanted feeling. The second way is to welcome the unwanted feeling, simply allowing the emotion to be. The third way is to dive into the very core of the emotion.

NLP (Neuro-Linguistic Programming)

NLP is a method of influencing brain behavior through the use of language and other types of communication to enable a person to "recode" the way the brain responds to situations. In essence, NLP provides practical ways to change the way you think, to adjust how you view past events and to encourage the manifestation of new and better behaviors.

PSYCH-K

Psych-K starts with the basis that we are *spiritual beings* having a *human experience*, and that when we align with this idea, we can be freed from a kind of prison of limiting beliefs and that the source of all suffering comes from the illusion that we are separated from the spiritual nature of who we truly are. PSYCH-K has various tools and processes for change derived from contemporary neuroscience research, as well as from ancient mind/body wisdom.

HYPNOSIS

Hypnosis is a natural state of selective, focused attention and is 100% natural. It requires us to enter a unique state of consciousness and access countless possibilities for healing, self-exploration and change. When we enter into the absorbed state of hypnosis, we can use our thoughts, talents and experiences in ways not usually available to us. With the help of a trained professional, we can develop our innate, individual abilities that enable us to make desired changes in our thoughts, feelings and behaviors.

BEHAVIORAL KINESIOLOGY

Behavioral Kinesiology assesses and evaluates the effects of all stimuli on the body – both internal and external – in order to arrive at a new understanding of the body energy system. The degree of stress under which a patient is functioning is assessed, and a rebalancing of the body energy is facilitated by showing the patient how to reduce stress and correct emotional attitudes. Behavioral Kinesiology is established on the basic philosophy of applied kinesiology: Every major muscle of the body relates to an organ, and these muscles and organs can be "tested" to determine the condition of the "life energy" flowing through the meridians related to them.

LET'S TAKE IT EVEN HIGHER

The great news is that as we remove these barriers from our subconscious, we change the energy around us and free our minds to generate and direct more positive thoughts toward whatever it is we choose to create. Kim Marcille Romaner talks about the concept of *amplification* in her book, *The Science of Making Things Happen.* She does a great job of explaining the key concepts and laws of quantum physics. She makes them understandable, especially as they relate to how our brains can work in symphony with these laws.

Romaner talks about the concept of *amplification*, the idea of beginning with something small and turning it into something much, much bigger:

> "There's a science to turning your desired possibilities into reality! The things we choose to bring into this reality are limited only by our imaginations. Our imaginations are limited only by our willingness to expand them. Why haven't you already brought your dreams to life? Is it because your dreams are not quite in focus? Do you hold back from getting a clear picture of what you want so that you won't end up disappointed in yourself or in life? Then learning how the brain amplifies even your smallest thought will inspire you."

> "Through amplification, you will learn how to accelerate the realization of your dreams and identify what you might be doing right now to slow yourself down."

> "You will begin to recognize the signs of this science at work as you transition from what used to be your "real" life to the life of your dreams. The universe is designed to make your possibilities come true. What happens at the quantum level of the universe can make a difference in your life. Take your dream and combine it with this science and make it happen!" (Romaner 177).

POSSIBILITY AMPLIFICATION PROCESS

In essence, Romaner's amplification process is all about choosing our own reality and not allowing the reality we choose to be limited. Romaner goes on to explain, "The truth is that the universe is made up of possibility. Through conscious and deliberate observation, we have the power to make the universe choose specific possibilities from all those available and amplify them into reality. This power is fundamental to the realization of our dreams, and it's a power every human being on the planet possesses. So why haven't we done this? Because we have been missing two necessary steps - awareness and the technology to access it." (Romaner).

She argues that there are two observers in our lives. The first is us as we observe ourselves. The second is the environment. It is our self-awareness, our ability to watch ourselves both in the present and in the future, that is the critical, initial step toward understanding who we really are and what we really want.

Romaner shares references to the work of Richard Feynman, Nobel Prize winning theoretical physicist. Based on his particle/wave experiments, Feynman references the physical rules that govern our everyday existence. He notes that observation modifies outcome. Essentially, he is saying that how we look at the universe influences the way the universe behaves.

"Forcing a subatomic particle to pick one specific possibility from all the different possibilities available," Romaner says, "can be achieved by very few forces of nature." She explains that one of these forces is observation. Observation can change the way subatomic particles behave. Therefore, because the universe is made up of subatomic particles and we are a part of the universe, *we can create or influence outcomes through the power of observation* (Romaner). Think about how powerful this could be in our own lives, no matter what it is we desire.

So what are the simplest ways for anyone to observe, become aware if and ultimately influence the universe?   The answer to that is through the process of first observing and then asking questions. Here are a few example questions:

- If I could feel confident and comfortable, what would that look like?
- If I did know the answer as to what is stopping me from presenting with confidence, what would it be?
- If I were totally passionate and having fun every time I presented to others, what would my life look like now?

The power of "if" questions can open up the forces of the universe at a subatomic level and trigger unlimited possibilities. Contrast this with the idea of starting your quest for possibility with self-defeating questions and self-imposed limitations, which can limit the answers you can get back from this process.

- Why can't I….
- Why is it so hard to stand in front of an audience….
- I never feel totally comfortable….

OBSERVATION AND VISUALIZATION:
In *The Science of Making Things Happen,* Romaner also recommends that we not only observe ourselves in the present, but that we also work to observe – to *visualize* – ourselves in our imaginations. She puts forth that visualization is a fundamental key on which the Possibility Amplification Process is built. It is a foundational piece of realizing our dreams. If we cannot vividly *see* what our success looks like, we will not achieve that success. It is only when we can imagine the reality of our dreams that the universe will deliver those dreams to us.

"So how can you tap into this great power" she asks? "Thinking – simple thinking – is the first component in the process by which our chaotic, iterative brains *amplify* raw, quantum possibility into reality. It is in the creation of a thought, the mere formulation of an idea, in which the process of possibility amplification begins" (Romaner).

The second part of the amplification process, according to Romaner, is choice. We must choose the ideas – the thoughts, visions and dreams – that we wish to see realized in our lives. She refers to the most recent developments in brain theory, proposing that our choices are the impetus to everything. What we choose to focus on is what we draw to us.

What we need to understand is that the quantum theory of brain activity is completely dependent on our intentions. That is, without an intention, without our *choosing* a preference, our brains cannot control our voluntary actions. Choice provides the personal power available to us in this amplification process.

"As you begin the amplification process, your thoughts, your actions and the environment around you may seem random and unpredictable. However, you must hold fast to your vision of what is to be. When you use your amplification power to choose the possibilities you want, you will begin to see patterns in the seeming randomness." (Romaner).

The act of visualizing – of vividly imagining what it is we want," she offers, "is an important key to making our dreams come true." She asks what I believe to be an important, eye-opening question: "How can the universe know what we want and offer it up, if we aren't clear ourselves?" (Romaner).

DESIGNING THE DESTINATION
It's important to note that as you begin to visualize what it is you want, it is essential to use very specific words to direct and truly leverage the subconscious mind, especially as you start to use the

amplification process. As we frame our thoughts, using terms like "desire" or "want" indicate to the subconscious mind that these things are *future-based*. Thus, the subconscious will not focus on nor direct energy effectively toward their creation. A more empowering or possibility-oriented phraseology would be "I *have* created" or "I *am* creating…."

An Additional Tool for Dealing with Blocks and Barriers

CORE MAP (Core Multidimensional Awareness Profile)

CORE MAP is an advanced assessment to help you discover how all your years of conditioning have altered the true self you came into the world to be and to help you quickly move past any negative conditioning so you can step out and shine authentically.

Some of the conditioning we receive as children is beneficial. It enhances our natural abilities. Some of it, though, (in fact, most of it for the majority of people) suppresses our natural abilities. Unless we can see what has been suppressed, we don't know what to work on. Many people spend an entire lifetime searching for their truth and die without ever knowing the joy of living their lives authentically.

This technique gets beneath the mask we don as children to unearth the core truth. When you know what your core truth is, you can step onto any stage or enter any arena feeling strong and confident. What you will learn about yourself and other people through CORE MAP can help you connect to and better understand any audience, and, more than that, it can connect you to the fullness of life. (You can learn more about CORE MAP at: https://energyofsuccess.net/processes/).

Creative Strategies for
Material Development and Presentation

Two of the biggest challenges most presenters wrestle with are creating valuable content and then putting that content into a logical and understandable format. Following are several strategies and processes I use to help me in the creation and organization of any presentation:

Tell 'Em

There is a familiar old adage that applies to public speaking: (1) Tell 'em what you're going to tell 'em, (2) Tell 'em, (3) Tell 'em what you told 'em. I have expanded that adage to include a few more steps in the process. This technique allows you to outline everything you need to do as you "tell 'em" what they need to know. Note: A little later on I will use these steps as a part of the Mind Mapping technique.

1. *Preparing what you need to tell 'em*
2. *Tell 'em what you're gonna tell 'em*
3. *Tell 'em*
4. *Telling 'em through speech*
5. *Telling 'em via facilitation*
6. *Telling 'em by training 'em*
7. *Motivating 'em as you tell 'em*
8. *Problems and mistakes in telling 'em*
9. *Tell 'em what you told 'em*
10. *Telling 'em after it's over and remind 'em later what you told 'em*

Mission Process

The Mission Process is a great way to gain the clarity you need before approaching an audience. In any given presentation, I have a specific mission that I want to accomplish on behalf of the audience. I have a specific reason for being there and specific information that I want to give to the audience to help them accomplish a task or goal. When I can clearly fill in these three blanks, I have the overall mission and focus of my presentation.

I help_____ do/understand _____
so they can _____.

A Framework for Anything

Brendon Burchard, author, high performance coach and founder of Experts Academy, advocates the use of a framework for any endeavor: to create a speech, to plan a training session, etc. His "Create a Framework for Anything" is a great template to follow because it's easy, it's understandable and it moves the audience toward a clear outcome. It also sets out a call to action, if that is your intention.

How Do I Make Sure They Understand and Remember?

Always use a framework.
A framework organizes your ideas.
A framework is teachable beyond you.
The framework is nameable, protectable and memorable.
A framework always answers a question.

How To Create A Framework For Anything

Here's who I am and what I do.
Have you ever had any of these challenges?
Me too! Here's my story of struggle.
Here's my story of finding the solution.
Here are the results – mine and others.

Here's the Old World versus the New World myth/trends.
Here's the solution, a step-by-step system in a framework.
Here are the most common mistakes - the DO's and the DON'Ts.
Here's the first thing to do once you finish my program.

(Note: You can access Brendon Burchard's free 50-minute training
video and "Create a Framework for Anything" here:
http://bit.ly/2rrRtJf).

Content Matrix
The following Content Matrix is a format I found recently. I suggest it because, if you're anything like me, you may have a tendency to try to include TOO much information. The key to this graph is to streamline and organize a body of information for your current and future programs.

The most essential information crucial to the development of our current program is the Must Know/Know Now box (highlighted). Ask yourself what is it that someone must know *now* to understand the message you're sharing. This is an easy, natural way to get any presentation down to the basics and to make sure you are identifying the most important items. Once you determine what those basics are, you can pull from the other parts of the graph to fill in as needed.

CONTENT MATRIX

	Must know	Should know	Nice to know
Know before			
Know now	**Fill Out First- Most Important**		
Know later			

Mind Mapping

Whether I'm working on a book, a speech or a full training course, I love the mind mapping process. It's a highly effective process that allows me to dump out the information in my brain in a non-linear fashion so it that can easily be changed to a more linear outline to accommodate the desired flow of the presentation:

Two key tools I use to create my Mind Maps:

- Inspiration – www.inspiration.com
- XMind – www.xmind.net

Below is an example of an Inspiration Mind Map

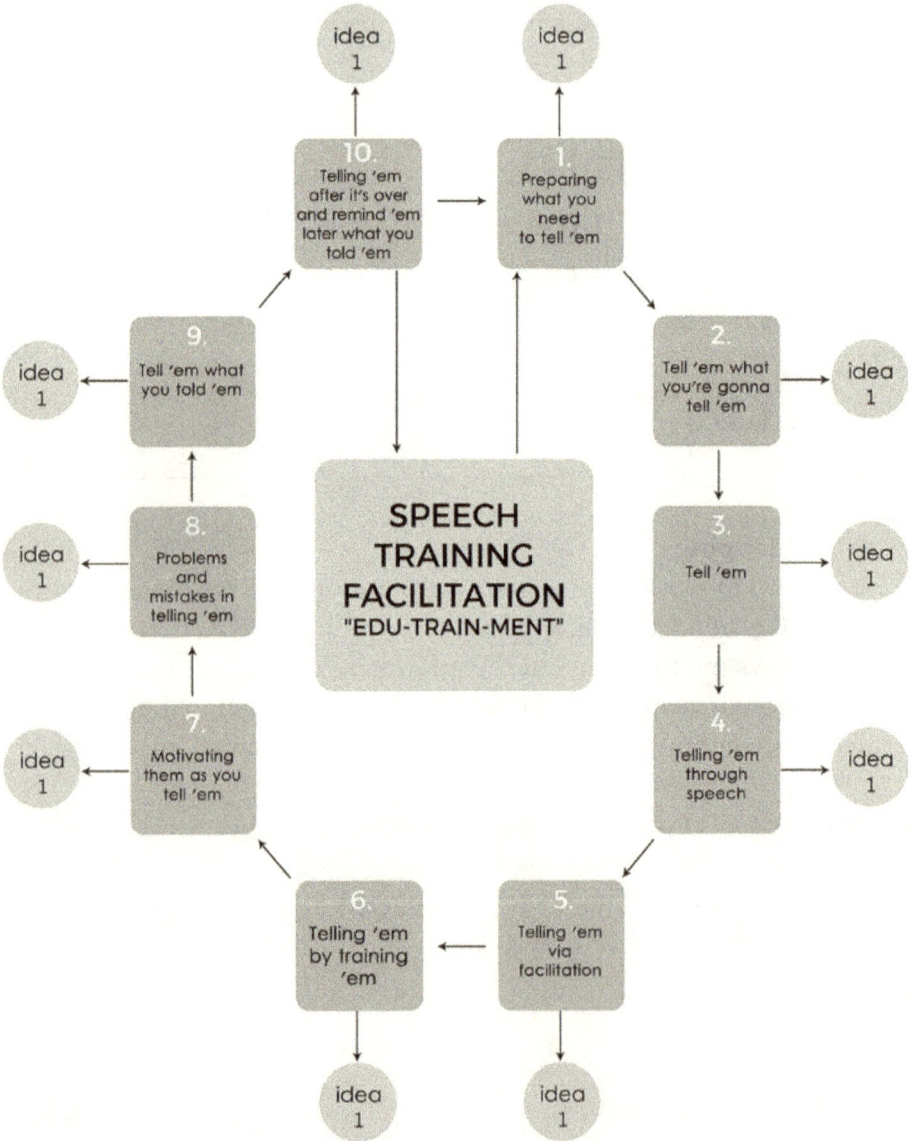

THE NO-FAIL FORMULA

Dr. Sherry Buffington describes a formula you can apply to everything you do – provided you follow it consistently – that absolutely guarantees you will not fail. This is called the "No-Fail" Formula. To use it, simply decide what you want to accomplish and then set out to make it happen in three simple steps:

- Attempt
- Assess
- Alter

First, make an *Attempt*. Once you've made the attempt, *Assess* your results. If your results are not exactly what you wanted, decide what might have gone wrong and make an *Alteration*. Once you have altered your course, go back and make another attempt. Assess the new results, and if you still don't get the desired results, make another alteration. Continue the process until you get the results you want, and you absolutely cannot fail. You may run out of life before you manage to achieve a really grand goal, but you won't have failed. You will just have run out of time. You will never fail as long as you continue to assess the reason you got the last result, make the adjustments and try again (Buffington, *The Law of Abundance*).

(Note: You can find Dr. Buffington's book here:
http://energyofsuccess.net/books/).

"NINETY PERCENT OF ALL THOSE WHO FAIL ARE NOT ACTUALLY DEFEATED. THEY SIMPLY QUIT."

John C. Maxwell

(Failing Forward: Turning Mistakes into Stepping Stones for Success)

(Note: To get *Failing Forward: Turning Mistakes into Stepping Stones for Success* by John C. Maxwell, visit: http://amzn.to/2kzZPe1).

Edu-Train-Ment™:

*It's important to provide your audience with powerful education and training, all while keeping them entertained. I learned this the hard way and below are some of my "hard-knocks" lessons that truly helped me understand the value of **Edu-Train-Ment™**. For now, simply ask yourself if your presentation, training and/or facilitation has the "**Edu-Train-Ment™**" factors it needs to make a difference.*

1. Are you educating your listeners about the possibilities and opportunities?
2. Are you training them to learn beyond their current skill levels?
3. Are you providing them memorable experiences and entertainment so they will retain the information better?

I'LL DO WHATEVER IT TAKES AS LONG AS IT'S NOT ILLEGAL, IMMORAL OR FATTENING.

I experienced one very challenging presentation that sticks in my mind to this day. I was doing a program with 70 managers at an aviation-related company. The president had been in constant communication with us prior to the program, sharing the messages he wanted conveyed. He took us on a tour of the facility and gave us access to himself, as well as to other key members of his team, so we could garner more specifics about how to customize the program. I was delighted with his enthusiasm and excited to jump into the session.

On the day of the presentation, the president sat at the very front table so everyone could see him. After he kicked off the meeting and introduced me, I was walking the room, connecting with the audience and setting the context for the day. About ten minutes in, I saw the president on the front row with his briefcase wide open and a newspaper held up in front of his face. I thought it was a joke and tried to ignore it, but it was tough to ignore him when he loudly turned the pages and shook the newspaper. It was very disrupting, and I could see that others in the room were equally baffled (and distracted) by his discourteous actions and the subliminal message he was sending.

Once he finished reading the newspaper, the president occupied himself with paperwork. He did not interact, engage or show one bit of interest in the training for which he had arranged and given his people a day away from work so they could attend.

This event took place very early in my speaking and training career, and the last thing I wanted to do was botch it by embarrassing the company president in front of his people. Nor did I want to dictate that he either lose the paper or remove himself from the room because he was sending a bad message to his team. I tolerated his behavior until the lunch break, at which point he came up to me and said that he did not think it was going well. Gulp. What a horrible feeling! He asked me to return after lunch and close out the program. I was forced to cut approximately three hours of material.

In the end, I had to leave out essential program information, and here is why I'm sharing this epic failure. It was a very powerful lesson, one that I learned from, and one I knew I NEVER wanted to experience again. To be totally authentic here, it scared me. It felt like I had let down the president and every manager in the room. I felt embarrassed and somewhat shameful. My internal talk became all about how I could have prepared more and/or how I lacked the presentation skills to make a real impact. That feeling and fear drove me to make a vow to myself to learn whatever I needed to learn and to do whatever I needed to do to always be engaging with the audience at the highest possible level.

From that moment on, I vowed always to couple my presentations with some level of fun and entertainment. That's when I coined the term Edu-Train-Ment™ and it has been my mantra ever since the day of that disastrous presentation.

Here's another personal story – let's say another lesson from my very own school of "hard knocks."

I was doing a multi-day training session for the sales managers of a company in Zurich, Switzerland. The group was a real cross-cultural mix. Although a select few struggled with the language, most participants were able to understand and speak English well. We were well into Day One, and the group and I were getting more comfortable with each other, which always seems to be the good *and* the bad news. I strive to create and actually crave a "container" of safety, which allows people to feel safe and to be authentic. It's energizing juice for me when I know that everyone is being "real," and in my experience, that kind of environment goes a long way in facilitating learning. The downside to a happy, comfortable group is that such a group can sometimes lose their sense of decorum and control. They can begin to talk, interrupt and defocus from the task at hand, which can severely impede the learning process.

On this particular day, the group was heading down the path of complacency, and as the Conductor of this Training Symphony, it was my responsibility to create and then control the environment of the room. Maintaining control of the room is an important role of every presenter so that those in attendance can get the desired results.

Over the years, I've learned that my subtle actions can be just as powerful, if not more powerful, than any overt move to interrupt an audience's distracting behaviors. So as the group talked rather than listened, I went to the front of the room and placed my foot on the front table. I put my chin in my hand and stood there without a word. About 45 seconds in, the group began to refocus on me. I continued to stand with my foot up as I scanned the group in silence. I could tell it was making them uncomfortable and nervous, but the energy of the room swung back in my direction. We had no more issues that day...except one.

It seems that putting my foot up on a table in front of the room was HIGHLY offensive to one of the women from Russia. It was so unnerving that for the rest of the day, she displayed very rebellious actions. She talked frequently to her fellow comrades from Russia, all while glancing at me and periodically pointing in my direction.

After the midday break, I pulled her aside and asked if everything was all right. She said "NO!" She told me that my actions of the morning were outrageous. She explained that in Russia doing with I did with my foot on the table was highly disrespectful and she was extremely offended. I told her I understood, explained that my gesture was not meant to be offensive and asked if she would be okay to let it go and come back into the flow of the group. She said she would try.

So, as Paul Harvey used to say, "Here's the rest of the story." The next day, each member of the group was assigned a "teach-back" in front of the room. When it came time for the Russian woman to present, I was blown away. She did an excellent job – probably the best of anyone in the room. Furthermore, when she was presenting, her English was clear and concise, with little of the deep Russian accent that was muffling her English communication the day before. In essence, she nailed it.

Afterwards, I congratulated her on an excellent presentation. She asked if she could speak openly with me, and I said, "Of course." She apologized for her outburst, overreaction and aggressive behavior of the previous day and proceeded to give me a bit more context about her as a person. It turns out she has a Ph.D. in organizational development in Russia and is very experienced as a presenter. She had only worked for the current company a short time and was still very uncomfortable in her role there. Then she said, "I know exactly why you put your foot on the table yesterday. I knew what you were doing. As a presenter and trainer myself, I use similar tactics. Even still, I could not get past the conditioning and reactions I have from my culture. This was not about you. My reaction was all about me, and for that I apologize."

WOW! She was articulate, smart, authentic and very personally aware. And as much as she took personal responsibility for her actions, I also walked away with an increased awareness and sensitivity of cultural differences and how they can affect the energy of a room or group.

TAKE THE FEEDBACK AND
NEVER LET 'EM GET YOU DOWN

My point in these two stories is that it's important to strive for Edu-Train-Ment™, no matter what happens. Even if someone steps up to criticize you, don't take it personally. Yes, I know it's sometimes easier said than done. Take the lesson you've learned and work to get better at your craft, but do not take it personally because then you might kill off that good, powerful and authentic voice inside you that is begging to be heard and has something very worthwhile to share.

"There is no such thing as failure, just feedback."
John C. Maxwell
(Failing Forward: Turning Mistakes into Stepping Stones for Success)

(Note: To get *Failing Forward: Turning Mistakes into Stepping Stones for Success* by John C. Maxwell, visit: http://amzn.to/2kzZPe1).

And be aware it is not the external people or circumstances that will thwart us in the long run. Rather, what limits us is our own historical conditioning and the negative voice that emanates from inside. The biggest issue you must deal with on your path to being a masterful presenter is that "voice". You know it. It has been a constant companion no matter how much skill and knowledge you've accumulated. It's the voice that has stopped you before, not just as a presenter but in other areas of your life as well. And now it's time to be rid of that voice once and for all.

The challenge is how to identify those blocks and get past them quickly so you can move on toward your lifetime dreams, goals and desires. The good news is that contained in this added Appendix is a list of proven strategies and techniques to help you get past your internal blocks. Remember, when you are ready and when you make the choice, *Success Is Just Around The Block*.

WORKS CITED

Andrews, M.A., Robert. "What is EMDR?" *EMDR Institute – Eye Movement Desensitization and Reprocessing Therapy.* http://emdr.com/what-is-emdr/. EMDR Institute, Inc., 2017. Web.

Baksa, Peter. "Can Our Brain Waves Affect Our Physical Reality?" *The Huffington Post.* http://www.thehuffingtonpost.com, 26 Sept. 2011. Web.

Buffington, S. D. *The Law of Abundance.* Dallas, TX: QuinStart Publishing, 2009. Print.

Buffington, Sherry. *Banish Blocks.* http://www.banishblocks.com. 2017. Web.

Burchard, Brendon. "Total Product Blueprint." http://totalproductblueprinttraining.com. 7 May 2011. Web.

Craig, Gary. "This is the Home for Official EFT™ (Emotional Freedom Techniques)." http://www.emofree.com. *English (US).* 2017. Web.

Henry, Richard Conn. "The Mental Universe." *Nature.* http://www.nature.com. Johns Hopkins University. Nature Publishing Group, 7 July 2005. Vol. 436. Web.

"Welcome to the Evolution of Consciousness." PSYCH-K Centre International. Nurturing Sacred Global Evolution. https://www.psych-k.com.The Myrddin Corporation, 2017. Web.

"Logosynthesis® Colorado." *Logosynthesis Colorado.*
http://logosynthesiscolorado.com. 2017. Web.

Ltd., XMind. "The Most Popular Mind Mapping Software on the
Planet." *XMind.* http://www.xmind.net. © XMind Ltd, 2006-2016.
Web.

Maxwell, John C. *Failing Forward: Turning Mistakes into Stepping
Stones for Success.* Thomas Nelson, 2000.   Print.

(NLP) Neuro Linguistic Programming Classes Dallas, Texas.
http://www.nlplearningsystems.com/index.htm. NLP Learning
Systems Corporation. Web.

Ortner, Nick. "Discover How to Use EFT Tapping, a Combination
of Ancient Chinese Acupressure and Modern Psychology, to Improve Your Health, Relationships, Level of Happiness, and Much
More...." *The Tapping Solution (EFT): How to Get Started*

https://www.thetappingsolution.com. The Tapping Solution, LLC,
2016. Web.

Poscente, Vince. "Episode 5: Becoming the Architect of Your Sub-
conscious." *Energy of Success by Marc Schwartz. Energy of Success
Podcast.* https:energyofsuccess.net/energy-success. Podcast/. 2017.
Web.

Poscente, Vince. *The Ant and the Elephant: Leadership for the Self: A
Parable and 5-Step Action Plan to Transform Workplace Performance.*
Embassy, 2006. Print.

Romaner, Kim Marcille. *The Science of Making Things Happen: Turn
Any Possibility into Reality.* Novato, CA: New World Library, 2010.
Print.

Schwartz, Marc. "Success Processes." *Energy of Success*.https://energyofsuccess.net/. 2017. Web.

"TATLife, The Home of the Tapas Acupressure Technique." *TATLife*. www.tat.life.com.TATLife, Inc., 2016. Web.

The Institute of Sports Performance. © www.tinssp.com.The Institute of Sports Performance, 2012-2015. Web.

The Sedona Method | Heal Yourself by Letting Go | Official Site. http://www.sedona.com/home/asp. Sedona Training Associates, 2017. Web.

"Visual Learning Overview." *Inspiration Software, Inc. - The Leader in Visual Thinking and Learning*. http://www.inspiration.com. 2017. Web.

Weiss, Laurie. *Letting it Go: Relieve Anxiety and Toxic Stress in Just a Few Minutes Using Only Words*. Littleton, CO: Empowerment Systems, 2016. Print.

Weiss, Laurie. *Quick Start Guide: Using Logosynthesis® to Release Anxiety, Stress and Worry*. https: www.booksbylaurie.com/guide. Web.

Youngblood, Mark. *Dear Human: Master your Emotions*. Inspire on Purpose, 2017. Print.

If you could have done it on your own by now, you would have!

Sometimes we need help.

BIO / PROGRAM INFORMATION / CONTACT

Marc Schwartz
Success Coach, Speaker, Trainer
Author & Entrepreneur

For over thirty years, Marc Schwartz has traveled the globe training and consulting with corporate leaders, managers, and sales professionals. He helps them identify and build on the intrinsic motivation that truly drives them to reach their best both personally and professionally. Additionally, he has trained whole teams and organizations on coaching, leadership and sales skills.

Marc also coaches corporate leaders, entrepreneurs and individuals who want accelerated results in their life. His coaching approach provides the education, resources and a highly refined process to guide these motivated people in identifying and developing their authentic self, as well as the real passion and purpose that will drive them toward their goals faster, better and easier.

Marc is a highly acclaimed speaker and trainer who actively engages the audience in his presentations through the use of experiential learning techniques. Groups regularly report Marc as high energy and able to have audiences laughing one minute and learning some powerful skills and life lessons the next.

Since 1988, Marc has built a successful consulting practice and several direct sales organizations. He has presented keynotes, seminars and workshops to over 50,000 people in thirty-eight countries on such topics as Generational Leadership, Coaching, Communication Styles, Sales, Key Account Management, Conflict Resolution and Team Development.

Marc is the co-author of *Power Shift*, a business book on how to lead the new generation workforce. Also he is the author of The Totally Engaged Audience, a book on fearless presentations. He has written multiple articles on: training effectiveness, coaching, leadership strategies, emotional intelligence, authentic selling, assessments and more fully engaging your workforce.

Marc has a BBA in Management and is certified as a Clinical Hypnotherapist, Corporate Coach, NLP Practitioner, CORE MAP Facilitator and RAMP (Rapidly Accelerated Mind Patterning) Practitioner.

PROGRAMS

- Power Shift™ - Discover What Happens When an Irresistible Force Meets an Influential Leader

- Exiting Oz - Generational Diversity and the Changing American Workforce

- A Leader's View of The New Workforce™

- The Totally Engaged Audience™

- Seven Essentials of Leadership™

- Leadership at The Core™

- 4S Conversations™ - Building Conversational Excellence

- Key Account Management – 4 Zone Selling™

- The Psychology of Superior Selling™

- Success Is Just Around The Block™

Power Shift: The New Rules of Engagement™
Keynote / Two to Four Hour Training Session /
One Day Workshop

Discover What Happens When an Irresistible Force Meets an Influential Leader (based on the soon-to-be-released book by Marc Schwartz and Dr. Sherry Buffington). Since the crash of 2008, learn why 72% of the working US population is either not engaged or actively disengaged in their jobs and why that may NOT change anytime soon unless we wake up to the changing workforce requirements.

Find out how to increase the interest and engagement levels of your workforce by creating an internal environment which is wholly attractive and compelling. Discover how and why the leaders within any organization hold the keys to reversing the trend of disengagement.

Clearly, companies with highly interested and highly engaged workers are more productive and more profitable, plus their customers are more satisfied and loyal. Employee engagement is the competitive edge we seek regardless of the product, service or industry.

Exiting Oz - Generational Diversity and the Changing American Workforce
Keynote / Two to Four Hour Training Session / One to Two Day Workshop

Exiting OZ is an eye-opening program about leadership, generational diversity and how organizations must shift their focus to survive in today's rapidly changing world. It is for owners, leaders, managers and team members interested in building a sustainable organization and populating it with dedicated, high performance people. These highly researched and groundbreaking strategies are also for high performance people interested in avoiding the perils and pitfalls of OZ organizations.

OZ is a metaphor for Organizational Zeal, and is depicted in Dr. Sherry Buffington's book, *Exiting OZ*, as the notion that the organization is more important than the people keeping it alive. OZ organizations are full of ineffective leaders and each is exposed in this book through clever comparisons to the characters from L. Frank Baum's book, *The Wonderful Wizard of Oz*.

Exiting OZ takes you on a fascinating journey through the world of typical organizations and explains in colorful analogies why business-as-usual is a formula for failure as the newer generations move into the workforce majority and reject standard management practices.

A Leader's View of The New Workforce™
Keynote / Two to Four Hour Training Session /
One to Two Day Workshop

This program focuses on the practical advice, skills and tools leaders and employees need to thrive in the new era of the multi-generational workforce. The goal is to increase awareness and provide strategies for the subtle differences happening every day with issues like work ethic, communication, career outlook, appearance and expectations.

In today's workplace where four generations work side by side, the potential for conflict, misunderstanding and even resentment is ever present. On the flip side, opportunities for productivity, creativity and knowledge transfer are equally as great if understanding and communication are the watchwords.

You probably notice subtle changes every day—differences in work ethic, communication, career outlook, expectations of bosses, retention factors, what keeps people engaged in their work—and on and on.

The game of business has changed; and when the game changes, the players need new rules. The New Game looks at talent through the generational lens. Our playbook is your guide to the changing workplace and what you can do to stay in the game.

The Totally Engaged Audience™
Three-Day Workshop

This three-day program will help you painlessly move to the next level as a presenter whether you are a beginner or a full-out professional. Day one, we will review *the 24 Unbreakable Rules of the Subconscious Mind* so you can overcome the three little known fears that keep most presenters from being truly powerful in front of any group. Further, we will review your CORE Assessment to determine your authentic style and discuss how to appeal to all CORE types in any audience. Additionally, you will go through a proven focus session to gain specific clarity on the presentation target you are moving toward to include the initial development of your powerful personal story. Day two and three will focus on the development of a specific presentation coupled with video reviews and coaching around these key points:

- Creating a powerful open and close

- Developing and integrating humorous stories and vignettes to support key points and build rapport
- Incorporation of your personal story to build undeniable connections to your audience

- Deeper work on the authentic "actor" in you to include using your three voices to engage a wider range of your audience all while having more FUN

- Practice recognized audience retention techniques that play to your natural style - EDU-TRAIN-MENT™

- Understand how to leverage the laws of physics to create the outcomes you want with any group

- Learn optimal balance points for speed, rate and pace of delivery to connect with what is most important to each audience

- Find out about the RAMP process that will get you past any barrier you have as a presenter

Seven Essentials of Leadership™
Keynote / Two to Four Hour Training Session /
One to Five Day Workshop

An influential leader's overview of the new workforce focuses on the practical advice, skills and tools leaders need to thrive in the new era of the multigenerational workforce. The goal is to increase awareness and provide strategies for the subtle differences that happen every day with issues like work ethic, communication, career outlook and expectations.

Leadership at The Core, Core PEP™ Profile
Keynote / Two to Four Hour Training Session /
One to Three Day Workshop

Use the highly acclaimed CORE profile to identify thinking and communication styles of self and others (co-workers and customers). Develop flexing strategies for improved conversations, coaching and leadership development…especially in the realm of a diverse multigenerational workforce.

4S Conversations™ - Foundation Program
Building Conversational Excellence
Keynote / Two to Four Hour Training Session /
One to Five Day Workshop

Managers face greater complexity in their role today than ever before and need to deliver results now. While many see the value in coaching and developing their people, often the perception is that they don't have the time to do so. Couple that with broader span of control and more employees to manage, interactions can default to a tell-oriented, point-and-direct experience. The result is that the same problems surface and need to be solved again and again, wasting precious time and effort.

The 4S Conversations® program provides a simple, scalable process for managers to coach and develop their people in the fast-paced market in which they compete. The program is designed to help leaders manage the talent on their teams through more focused and strategic conversations. The goal is for every manager-employee interaction to build a culture of continuous improvement and trust while driving toward success.

By participating in the *4S Conversations® - Foundation* workshop, managers will:

- Significantly improve the quality of their work relationships

- Achieve targets more consistently

- Foster a spirit of accountability at the employee/peer level

- Increase the impact of existing organizational performance communication tools/processes and training

- Invest the right amount in both performance management and individual development

- Build high value trusting relationships

- Provide a forum to address the unique challenges of their people

Key Account Management - The 4-Zone Selling Process™
Keynote / Two to Four Hour Training Session /
One to Two Day Workshop

The 4-Zone Account Selling Workshop contains the overall structure, key insights, techniques and approaches that you can leverage to create more customer-centric relationships within your current and future accounts.

As you work both individually and in a team setting with the content in this program, you will become familiar with each of the 4 "Zones" and the role they play in helping you generate effective account strategies and more meaningful dialogue with each of your account stakeholders.

The 4 Zones™ is a time-tested, proven account-selling model, and when utilized properly, allows you to advance more simultaneous opportunities in your accounts by having better information and access.

The Psychology of Superior Selling™
Keynote / Two to Four Hour Training Session /
One to Two Day Workshop

Outstanding salespeople have some very specific attributes which go beyond technique and which make them many times more effective than most.

While technical training provides good basic selling skills, technique alone cannot produce outstanding performers. In fact, the very attributes that make salespeople great can also cause them to resist using many of the traditional techniques generally taught in sales training sessions.

Master sellers instinctively know which technique will work best with different customer types. They can instantly pick up on clues telling them what type of customer they are dealing with and can then adjust their approach, presentation, and closing style to fit the needs of the customer.

These powerful, moneymaking processes can be learned and incorporated by almost any salesperson. Even seasoned professionals will discover new and innovative ways to improve their outcomes.

Through a series of profiles, interactive exercises, and actual on-the-job applications, participants learn and internalize skills that produce dramatic results. This workshop takes ordinary sales people to new heights of success and makes superstars of the already effective ones.

Success Is Just Around the Block™
Keynote / Two to Four Hour Training Session /
One to Four Day Workshop

Understand how the *24 Unbreakable Rules of the Subconscious Mind* and the irrefutable laws of physics can be combined to create one of the greatest forces on the planet for human accomplishment. Hear about the deep research that is emerging, such that humans can create predictable and repeatable abundance in any aspect of life by increased awareness around these rules and laws.

PROCESSES

CORE MAP (CORE Multidimensional Awareness Profile)

This is an advanced assessment to help you discover how all the years of conditioning have altered the true self you came into the world to be and quickly move you past any negative conditioning so you can step out and shine authentically. Some of the conditioning we receive as children is beneficial. It enhances our natural abilities. Some of it, in fact, most of it for the majority of people, suppresses our natural abilities and unless we can see what has been suppressed and what has not, we don't know what to work on. Many people spend an entire lifetime searching for their truth and die without ever knowing the joy of living their life authentically. CORE MAP gets beneath the mask we don as children and gets to the core truth. When you know what your core truth is, you can step onto any stage or enter any arena stronger and more confident. What you will learn about yourself and other people through CORE MAP can help you connect to and better understand any audience. More than that, it can connect you to the fullness of life. You can learn more about CORE MAP at www.energyofsuccess.net.

RAMP (Rapidly Accelerated Mind Patterning)

If fear or anxiety is what prevents you from stepping out there and doing what you want to do, nothing will eliminate either or both of them faster or more completely than RAMP. This is a method that is almost 100% effective in removing limitations and knocking out mental or emotional blocks that keep you stuck. RAMP can accomplish more in a single hour than other methods accomplish in months, or even years. RAMP works even where "tried and true" methods, such as traditional therapy, have failed. The transformation is immediate and once a desired change is made through the RAMP method, it occurs effortlessly and remains permanently. After RAMP, people regularly report that where their automatic responses used to frustrate them, they now delight in them. That's the power of this amazing method. To learn more about RAMP, go to www.energyofsuccess.net.

For More Information About Any of Our Programs or Processes Go To:
www.energyofsuccess.net/programs

www.ingramcontent.com/pod-product-compliance
Lightning Source LLC
Chambersburg PA
CBHW031318040426
42443CB00005B/120